Endorsements for
Keep Start Stop & Deliver – An Active Devotional

"*Keep, Start, Stop, and Deliver: An Active Devotional* by Todd Crippin is a great guide for those seeking to truly integrate God's wisdom into their daily lives. By applying the innovative KSSD method to Scripture, this devotional challenges readers to move beyond passive reflection and engage in active spiritual growth, fostering a deeper, more lasting connection with God's teachings. It's an approach I haven't seen before, and I'm excited to integrate it into my daily time with God."

– Jordan Raynor, bestselling author of
The Sacredness of Secular Work **and** *Redeeming Your Time*

"Todd's inspiration for creating his *Keep, Start, Stop, Deliver* devotional is truly exceptional and revolutionizes the traditional approach to devotionals. Rather than a mere paragraph or two of praise for the day's verse, Todd has crafted a comprehensive structure that can be applied to any passage in God's Word. This framework challenges us not only to continue our actions in accordance with the specific scripture, but also prompts us to take on new actions based on the weekly scripture. Notably, it goes beyond simply maintaining current practices or initiating new ones — it also urges us to cease behaviors that contradict the guidance provided by the scripture. Most importantly, we are motivated to deliver on God's Word by faithfully committing ourselves to implementing its teachings into our lives. Without a doubt, Todd's devotional should be an essential tool for any accountability partner as it presents a natural framework for meaningful discussions about God's Word and how we can apply it in practical ways within our daily lives."

– Greg Atchinson, Principal Chair, C12 of Greater St. Louis

"When Jesus commissioned his followers, he highlighted the importance of teaching disciples to obey everything he commanded. There is something about applying and practicing what the Bible teaches that is essential to following Jesus. It is too easy to settle for increased knowledge or new spiritual insight alone in our devotional lives. In *Keep Start Stop Deliver —An Active Devotional*, Todd Crippin invites readers to move beyond these experiences to an active response to God's Word. I am confident that this way of interacting with God's Word will result in deep spiritual intimacy and real-life change, which is what God wants to do in your life."

– John Richardson, Executive Pastor of Discipleship,
First Free Church, Manchester, MO

"Like many people, I have often struggled to consistently stay focused on Bible studies. The busyness of life presses down, and I find myself unable to keep up with the rigor of daily studies. *Keep, Start, Stop, and Deliver* is different from any other daily devotional I've read, though. Each week forces you to slow down and meditate on a single verse while answering very practical prompts that give you action items on which to focus. By the end of the week, you will not only have engaged with the Word, but you very likely will have memorized the verses as well. This is the daily devotional we all never knew we needed!"

– Kelli Stuart, Author of Life Creative: Inspiration for Today's Renaissance Mom and The Master Craftsman.

"Todd Crippin's *Keep, Start, Stop, Deliver* offers a transformative approach to integrating faith with professional practice. By utilizing the powerful exercise of Keep, Start, Stop, and Deliver, this devotional provides a clear and actionable plan for flourishing in our daily walk with the Lord. Having presented this concept at our men's breakfast, where over 50 men were encouraged by it, Todd's method is both tried and true, making it an essential guide for anyone seeking to live out God's Word in practical, impactful ways in their career and beyond."

– Ryan Kapple, Senior Pastor, Leawood Presbyterian Church, Leawood, KS

"Todd offers an exceptional approach to devotions with his use of the KSSD method, adapting a business world practice to biblical studies. This technique enables individuals to meditate on, understand, and apply biblical content effectively."

– Dr. Benjamin J. Wendt
Vice Chairman of Bridge The Globe & Vice President at First Citizens Bank

KEEP START
STOP DELIVER

An Active Devotional

TODD CRIPPIN

Keep, Start, Stop, and Deliver
An Active Devotional
Todd Crippin

JMH
Justice Mercy Humility
PUBLISHING

Published by JMH Publishing, Overland Park, Kansas

Project Management and Book Design: Davis Creative Publishing, DavisCreativePublishing.com

Editor: Kimberly Fletcher

Library of Congress Cataloging-in-Publication Data
(Provided by Cassidy Cataloguing Services, Inc.)
Names: Crippin, Todd, author.
Title: Keep start stop deliver : an active devotional / Todd Crippin.
Description: Overland Park, Kansas : JMH Publishing, [2024]
Identifiers: ISBN: 979-8-9906241-0-8 (paperback) | LCCN: 2024910208
Subjects: LCSH: Devotional exercises. | Devotional calendars. | Bible--Study and teaching. | Christian life. | Word of God (Christian theology) | LCGFT: Devotional literature. | BISAC: RELIGION / Devotional.
Classification: LCC: BV4832.3 .C75 2024 | DDC: 242--dc23

Dedication

To Renée, Audrey, and Claire–
This began as my legacy to you, and
your love and generosity has made it
so much more. May God bless you and
keep you all.

Table of Contents

INTRODUCTION

I have read devotions and the verse of the day for as long as I can remember. Many of them cause me to reflect on how God operates in my life and how I respond to Him. Unfortunately, these reflections often end as soon as I close my devotional or Bible. If I'm lucky, I might think about the words once or twice later in the day and offer a quick prayer to God. But I want more. I don't want to read a devotion or a Scripture out of habit, but witness no real change. Instead, I want to read, and then permanently incorporate God's wisdom and inspiration into my life.

One day, I remembered an exercise from my professional career that helped me decide what to *Keep, Start,* and *Stop (KSS)* for a business process. Adding KSS to my assignments made me think about how to engage and actively work to pursue solutions. So, I decided to try an experiment. What if I reviewed my favorite Bible verses and applied the KSS system to them? Could I read a verse and think about it in terms of what God is calling me to *keep, start,* and *stop* doing? And what if I put one more step in the process—*deliver*? How will I *deliver* on my KSS promises? Maybe I change a practice or simply pray for wisdom and discernment to find out the "how."

Those were the thoughts that birthed what you're now holding in your hands—*Keep, Start, Stop, and Deliver: An Active Devotional*. At first, I envisioned a quarterly journal with a new verse every day. But as I shared my concept with others and prayed about it, I ended up with a 52-week devotional. Good thing, because I know myself well enough to admit that I wouldn't have the stamina to develop a KSS (and D) promise for every day of the year. Instead, I decided to spread each KSSD over a week as outlined on the Instructions page.

I mentioned that this devotional is an experiment, and as such, I would love to receive your feedback. Your praises, questions, concerns, and general thoughts are welcome and encouraged. I genuinely look forward to hearing from you. To leave a comment, visit @activedevotionals1965 on YouTube or activedevotional.com. I will post videos sharing my own thoughts and takeaways as I walk through this experiment with you.

Thank you for your purchase. I hope we can all grow in God's love—for Him and for each other. Now, let us *Keep, Start, Stop, and Deliver*…and feel the power of Scripture.

INSTRUCTIONS

To get the most out of this devotional, I encourage you to follow this outline:

Day 1: **KEEP**
- Meditate on the verse of the week at least 3 times during the day.
- List a minimum of 2 actions you will **KEEP** doing based on the meaning of the verse.

Day 2: **START**
- Meditate on the verse of the week at least 3 times during the day.
- List a minimum of 2 actions you will **START** doing based on the meaning of the verse.

Day 3: **STOP**
- Meditate on the verse of the week at least 3 times during the day.
- List a minimum of 2 actions you will **STOP** doing based on the meaning of the verse.

Day 4: **DELIVER**
- Meditate on the verse of the week at least 3 times during the day.
- Review days 1-3. Choose 1 KEEP statement, 1 START statement, and 1 STOP statement. Write down how you will **DELIVER** on each of these statements.

Day 5: **PRACTICE**
- Meditate on the verse of the week at least 3 times during the day.
- Complete the **PRACTICE SCRIPTURE** activities.

Day 6: **REFLECT**
- Meditate on the verse of the week at least 3 times during the day.
- **REFLECT** on days 1-5. Write down how this week and previous weeks have impacted you.
- Write down the Bible verse from memory.

Day 7: **REST**

A SAMPLE WEEK

Below is a sample entry to help you understand how to use and get the most out of the *Keep, Start, Stop, and Deliver* devotional.

DAY 1

> *And I heard the voice of the Lord saying, "Whom shall I send, and who will go for us?"*
> *Then I said, "Here I am! Send me."*
> Isaiah 6:8

KEEP: During my quiet time with God, I will listen in my prayers and Scripture reading for his voice. Listen to the world around me. Listen to my spouse, my children, family, friends, and co-workers. I must understand that God may not be sending me overseas on a mission trip, but he has called me to be a spiritual leader for those around me.

DAY 2

> *And I heard the voice of the Lord saying, "Whom shall I send, and who will go for us?"*
> *Then I said, "Here I am! Send me."*
> Isaiah 6:8

START: I must begin to prepare myself for whatever God's calling is for me. I can do this by looking for opportunities within my church and community. I'll talk with others who have followed God's call and learn how they discerned his calling. He equips us with different spiritual gifts, and I must determine how he has equipped me.

DAY 3

> *And I heard the voice of the Lord saying, "Whom shall I send, and who will go for us?"*
> *Then I said, "Here I am! Send me."*
> Isaiah 6:8

STOP: I have to stop the lies of the enemy from keeping me from coming forth and say to God, "Here I am! Send me." I need to quit thinking God will call me to something bigger than I can handle. Why would he call me to a mission only to fail him? Every call from him is a call from grace and to a place where I can serve him.

DAY 4

> *And I heard the voice of the Lord saying, "Whom shall I send, and who will go for us?"*
> *Then I said, "Here I am! Send me."*
> Isaiah 6:8

DELIVER: During my time reading my Bible and praying, I will ask him where he is sending me and then I will LISTEN. Read and re-read 1 Kings 19:11-13 to understand that God does not always speak to us in the big moments (hurricanes, earthquakes, and fire), but many times in the small whisper of the night. I need to slow my life down and detach from the frantic pace so I can hear God speak to me.

DAY 5

And I heard the voice of the Lord saying, "Whom shall I send, and who will go for us?"
Then I said, "Here I am! Send me."

Isaiah 6:8

Put into practice the Keep, Start, Stop, and Deliver action items you developed over the past four days based on Isaiah 6:8.

PRACTICE SCRIPTURE:

I heard the voice of the Lord

1. Have you ever heard the Lord speak to you audibly or within your heart?
   a. If so, recall that time and write down what God relayed to you.
   b. If not, what do you think you can do to hear God?

Here I am! Send me

1. Does it frighten you to say these words to God and to wait for his reply? Reflect on this fear and decide what you will do to cast it aside.
2. Where will you go for God? Are you willing to travel to another country, go someplace new in your city, or share your faith in your home?
3. Pray and listen to God for 2 places you can spread the gospel through your actions and words, and go.

DAY 6

And I heard the voice of the Lord saying, "Whom shall I send, and who will go for us?"
Then I said, "Here I am! Send me."

Isaiah 6:8

Reflect on how you incorporated Isaiah 6:8 into your life this week, and assess your spiritual growth over the previous weeks. Write this week's verse from memory.

REFLECT: I am making a concentrated effort to listen for God. Working to listen for him without falling asleep or having my mind wander. Thought quite a bit about the armor of God as Paul describes in Ephesians 6:10-18 as a way to keep the fears I have from becoming deeply rooted in me. I listened to the song "Fear is a Liar" by Zach Williams and found comfort in this.

I have begun to consider what my spiritual gifts are. I've looked at various resources to help me determine my gifts. I even took a few spiritual gift surveys to see where I land. Want to use these outcomes to help me guide my prayers, and ask God to use me and my gifts to go where he will send me. Honestly, I'm afraid every step of the way.

And I heard the voice of the Lord saying, "Whom shall I send, and who will go for us?" Then I said, "HERE I AM! SEND ME." Isaiah 6:8

ENJOY GOD'S REST ON DAY 7

WEEK 1 – DAY 1

And let us consider how to stir up one another to love and good works.
Hebrews 10:24

KEEP: _____

_____

_____

_____

_____

_____

_____

WEEK 1 – DAY 2

And let us consider how to stir up one another to love and good works.
Hebrews 10:24

START:_____

_____

_____

_____

_____

_____

_____

_____

_____

WEEK 1 – DAY 3

And let us consider how to stir up one another to love and good works.
Hebrews 10:24

STOP: _____

_____

_____

_____

_____

_____

_____

_____

WEEK 1 – DAY 4

And let us consider how to stir up one another to love and good works.
Hebrews 10:24

DELIVER: _____

_____

_____

_____

_____

_____

_____

_____

_____

WEEK 1 – DAY 5

And let us consider how to stir up one another to love and good works.

Hebrews 10:24

Put into practice the Keep, Start, Stop, and Deliver action items you developed over the past four days based on Hebrews 10:24.

PRACTICE SCRIPTURE:

Consider how to stir up one another

1. Attend church, a bible study, a men's group, a women's group, etc.
2. Talk with your best friend, and discuss how the two of you can become accountability partners for each other.

To love

3. Do something for someone else without them asking.
4. Spend at least thirty minutes participating in an activity with someone you love (e.g., spouse, children, sibling, aging parent, best friend, etc.).

And good works

5. Give time to your church or favorite charity.
6. List ways you can please and glorify God through your work.

_____

_____

_____

_____

_____

_____

_____

_____

_____

_____

_____

_____

_____

_____

_____

_____

_____

_____

_____

_____

_____

_____

WEEK 1 – DAY 6

And let us consider how to stir up one another to love and good works.

Hebrews 10:24

Reflect on how you incorporated Hebrews 10:24 into your life this week, and assess your spiritual growth over the previous weeks. Write this week's verse from memory.

REFLECT: _____

_____

_____

_____

_____

_____

_____

ENJOY GOD'S REST ON DAY 7

WEEK 2 – DAY 1

For God gave us a spirit not of fear but of power and love and self-control.
2 Timothy 1:7

KEEP: _____

_____

_____

_____

_____

_____

_____

_____

WEEK 2 – DAY 2

For God gave us a spirit not of fear but of power and love and self-control.
2 Timothy 1:7

START:_____

_____

_____

_____

_____

_____

_____

_____

_____

WEEK 2 – DAY 3

For God gave us a spirit not of fear but of power and love and self-control.
2 Timothy 1:7

STOP: _____

_____

_____

_____

_____

_____

_____

_____

WEEK 2 – DAY 4

For God gave us a spirit not of fear but of power and love and self-control.
2 Timothy 1:7

DELIVER: _____

_____

_____

_____

_____

_____

_____

_____

_____

WEEK 2 – DAY 5

For God gave us a spirit not of fear but of power and love and self-control.
2 Timothy 1:7

Put into practice the Keep, Start, Stop, and Deliver action items you developed over the past four days based on 2 Timothy 1:7.

PRACTICE SCRIPTURE:

Spirit not of fear
1. Pray for God to deliver you from fear, anxiety, and worry.
2. Download a meditation app.
3. Read about Jesus' death and resurrection to understand how his sacrifice will help you conquer fear and timidity, including fear of death, because Jesus overcame it all.

Spirit of power and love
4. Learn someone's love language.

Spirit of self-control
5. Turn over your sins to God, and ask the Holy Spirit to bring Christlike attitudes and actions into your life. The Holy Spirit is given to you when you accept Christ as your Lord and Savior.
6. Make a list of your current desires or wants, and work to understand the motivation behind those desires.

_____

_____

_____

_____

_____

_____

_____

_____

_____

_____

_____

_____

_____

_____

_____

_____

_____

_____

_____

_____

_____

WEEK 2 – DAY 6

For God gave us a spirit not of fear but of power and love and self-control.
2 Timothy 1:7

Reflect on how you incorporated 2 Timothy 1:7 into your life this week, and assess your spiritual growth over the previous weeks. Write this week's verse from memory.

REFLECT: _____

_____

_____

_____

_____

_____

ENJOY GOD'S REST ON DAY 7

WEEK 3 – DAY 1

Therefore, confess your sins to one another and pray for one another, that you may be healed. The prayer of a righteous person has great power as it is working.
James 5:16

KEEP: _____

_____

_____

_____

_____

_____

_____

_____

WEEK 3 – DAY 2

Therefore, confess your sins to one another and pray for one another, that you may be healed. The prayer of a righteous person has great power as it is working.
James 5:16

START:_____

_____

_____

_____

_____

_____

_____

_____

_____

WEEK 3 – DAY 3

Therefore, confess your sins to one another and pray for one another, that you may be healed. The prayer of a righteous person has great power as it is working.

James 5:16

STOP: _____

_____

_____

_____

_____

_____

_____

WEEK 3 – DAY 4

Therefore, confess your sins to one another and pray for one another, that you may be healed. The prayer of a righteous person has great power as it is working.

James 5:16

DELIVER: _____

_____

_____

_____

_____

_____

_____

_____

WEEK 3 – DAY 5

Therefore, confess your sins to one another and pray for one another, that you may be healed. The prayer of a righteous person has great power as it is working.
James 5:16

Put into practice the Keep, Start, Stop, and Deliver action items you developed over the past four days based on James 5:16.

PRACTICE SCRIPTURE:

Confess your sins to one another
1. Spend time with God and confess your sins.
2. Ask God to connect you with a trustworthy confidante of the same sex who you can confess your sins to.

Pray for one another, that you may be healed
3. Ask your trusted friend to join you in writing out your sins on a piece of paper. Pray for freedom from the sins, and then tear up your list and throw it away.
4. Too often we pray for our community, but neglect to pray with our community. Take time to pray with your community, which includes your spouse, family, and friends. Pray for forgiveness, healing (emotionally, physically, and spiritually), and whatever else the Holy Spirit lays upon your heart.

As it is working
5. Keep a record of the sin that weighs heaviest on your heart. As you confess your sin and pray for your cleansing, keep track of how this sin is relinquishing its hold on you.
6. You and your trusted friend can serve as accountability partners to help each other avoid slipping into old, sinful habits. At each accountability session, discuss how your lives are changing.

_____

_____

_____

_____

_____

_____

_____

_____

_____

_____

_____

_____

_____

_____

_____

_____

_____

_____

_____

WEEK 3 – DAY 6

Therefore, confess your sins to one another and pray for one another, that you may be healed. The prayer of a righteous person has great power as it is working.
James 5:16

Reflect on how you incorporated James 5:16 into your life this week, and assess your spiritual growth over the previous weeks. Write this week's verse from memory.

REFLECT: _____

_____

_____

_____

ENJOY GOD'S REST ON DAY 7

WEEK 4 – DAY 1

Blessed be the God and Father of our Lord Jesus Christ, the Father of mercies and God of all comfort, who comforts us in all our affliction, so that we may be able to comfort those who are in any affliction, with the comfort with which we ourselves are comforted by God.
2 Corinthians 1:3-4

KEEP: _____

_____

_____

_____

_____

_____

_____

_____

WEEK 4 – DAY 2

Blessed be the God and Father of our Lord Jesus Christ, the Father of mercies and God of all comfort, who comforts us in all our affliction, so that we may be able to comfort those who are in any affliction, with the comfort with which we ourselves are comforted by God.
2 Corinthians 1:3-4

START: _____

_____

_____

_____

_____

_____

_____

WEEK 4 – DAY 3

Blessed be the God and Father of our Lord Jesus Christ, the Father of mercies and God of all comfort, who comforts us in all our affliction, so that we may be able to comfort those who are in any affliction, with the comfort with which we ourselves are comforted by God.
2 Corinthians 1:3-4

STOP: _____

_____

_____

_____

_____

_____

_____

_____

WEEK 4 – DAY 4

Blessed be the God and Father of our Lord Jesus Christ, the Father of mercies and God of all comfort, who comforts us in all our affliction, so that we may be able to comfort those who are in any affliction, with the comfort with which we ourselves are comforted by God.
2 Corinthians 1:3-4

DELIVER: _____

_____

_____

_____

_____

_____

_____

_____

WEEK 4 – DAY 5

Blessed be the God and Father of our Lord Jesus Christ, the Father of mercies and God of all comfort, who comforts us in all our affliction, so that we may be able to comfort those who are in any affliction, with the comfort with which we ourselves are comforted by God.
2 Corinthians 1:3-4

Put into practice the Keep, Start, Stop, and Deliver action items you developed over the past four days based on 2 Corinthians 1:3-4.

PRACTICE SCRIPTURE:

Who comforts us in all affliction
1. Pray for comfort, and ask God to surround you with his arms so our Savior can lighten your burdens and deliver you.
2. Reflect on a time when you suffered, and think about how you made it through the affliction.

We may be able to comfort those who are in any affliction
3. Serve in some capacity of pastoral care at your church (e.g., prayer team, communion to the homebound, hospitality for recovery groups, etc.).
4. Donate your resources to a recovery charity or people group of your choice. For example, you could donate your time or money to a women's shelter or a prison ministry.

With the comfort with which we ourselves are comforted by God
5. Reflect on how you have been comforted by God, and apply those ways to the individuals and groups you identified in the previous section.
6. Spend 5-10 minutes offering a prayer of thanksgiving to God. Read Psalms 30 and 100.

_____

_____

_____

_____

_____

_____

_____

_____

_____

_____

_____

_____

_____

_____

_____

_____

WEEK 4 – DAY 6

Blessed be the God and Father of our Lord Jesus Christ, the Father of mercies and God of all comfort, who comforts us in all our affliction, so that we may be able to comfort those who are in any affliction, with the comfort with which we ourselves are comforted by God.
2 Corinthians 1:3-4

Reflect on how you incorporated 2 Corinthians 1:3-4 into your life this week, and assess your spiritual growth over the previous weeks. Write this week's verses from memory.

REFLECT: _____

_____

_____

_____

_____

_____

ENJOY GOD'S REST ON DAY 7

WEEK 5 – DAY 1

Be obedient to God, and do not allow your lives to be shaped by those desires you had when you were still ignorant. Instead, be holy in all that you do, just as God who called you is holy.
1 Peter 1:14-15 (GNT)

KEEP: _____

_____

_____

_____

_____

_____

_____

_____

WEEK 5 – DAY 2

Be obedient to God, and do not allow your lives to be shaped by those desires you had when you were still ignorant. Instead, be holy in all that you do, just as God who called you is holy.
1 Peter 1:14-15 (GNT)

START: _____

_____

_____

_____

_____

_____

_____

_____

WEEK 5 – DAY 3

Be obedient to God, and do not allow your lives to be shaped by those desires you had when you were still ignorant. Instead, be holy in all that you do, just as God who called you is holy.
1 Peter 1:14-15 (GNT)

STOP: _____

_____

_____

_____

_____

_____

_____

WEEK 5 – DAY 4

Be obedient to God, and do not allow your lives to be shaped by those desires you had when you were still ignorant. Instead, be holy in all that you do, just as God who called you is holy.
1 Peter 1:14-15 (GNT)

DELIVER: _____

_____

_____

_____

_____

_____

_____

_____

WEEK 5 – DAY 5

Be obedient to God, and do not allow your lives to be shaped by those desires you had when you were still ignorant. Instead, be holy in all that you do, just as God who called you is holy.
1 Peter 1:14-15 (GNT)

Put into practice the Keep, Start, Stop, and Deliver action items you developed over the past four days based on 1 Peter 1:14-15.

PRACTICE SCRIPTURE:

Be obedient to God
1. What does "obedience to God" mean to you?
2. Find verses in the Old Testament and the New Testament that speak to you about obedience to God.

Be holy in all that you do
3. What does "holy" mean to you?
4. How does your definition of holy impact all that you do?

Just as God who called you is holy
5. Discover the attributes of God (suggested reading, The Attributes of God by A.W. Tozer).
6. Why is it important that God is holy?

_____

_____

_____

_____

_____

_____

_____

_____

_____

_____

_____

_____

_____

_____

_____

_____

_____

_____

_____

WEEK 5 – DAY 6

Be obedient to God, and do not allow your lives to be shaped by those desires you had when you were still ignorant. Instead, be holy in all that you do, just as God who called you is holy.
1 Peter 1:14-15 (GNT)

Reflect on how you incorporated 1 Peter 1:14-15 into your life this week, and assess your spiritual growth over the previous weeks. Write this week's verses from memory.

REFLECT: _____

_____

_____

_____

_____

_____

ENJOY GOD'S REST ON DAY 7

WEEK 6 – DAY 1

And let the peace of Christ rule in your hearts, to which indeed you
were called in one body. And be thankful.
Colossians 3:15

KEEP: _____

_____

_____

_____

_____

_____

_____

WEEK 6 – DAY 2

And let the peace of Christ rule in your hearts, to
which indeed you were called in one body. And be thankful.
Colossians 3:15

START:_____

_____

_____

_____

_____

_____

_____

_____

WEEK 6 – DAY 3

And let the peace of Christ rule in your hearts,
to which indeed you were called in one body. And be thankful.
Colossians 3:15

STOP: _____

_____

_____

_____

_____

_____

_____

WEEK 6 – DAY 4

And let the peace of Christ rule in your hearts,
to which indeed you were called in one body. And be thankful.
Colossians 3:15

DELIVER: _____

_____

_____

_____

_____

_____

_____

_____

WEEK 6 – DAY 5

And let the peace of Christ rule in your hearts, to which indeed
you were called in one body. And be thankful.
Colossians 3:15

Put into practice the Keep, Start, Stop, and Deliver action items you developed over the past four days based on Colossians 3:15.

PRACTICE SCRIPTURE:

And let the peace of Christ rule in your hearts
1. What does having a "peaceful heart" mean to you?
2. Pray for the peace of Christ to abide in your heart prior to a situation that you know will aggravate or frustrate you. After you pray, see if you notice a difference in your attitude or conduct.

Called in one body
3. Why is it important for the body of Christian believers to have a peaceful heart as a whole—toward believers and non-believers alike?
4. If you don't attend a church, go online to find one or receive a referral from a friend. Visit the church at least once.

And be thankful
5. Make a list of the things you are thankful for.
6. Say "thank you" to everyone who does something for you today, including God.

_____

_____

_____

_____

_____

_____

_____

_____

_____

_____

_____

_____

_____

_____

_____

_____

_____

_____

_____

_____

WEEK 6 – DAY 6

And let the peace of Christ rule in your hearts,
to which indeed you were called in one body. And be thankful.
Colossians 3:15

Reflect on how you incorporated Colossians 3:15 into your life this week,
and assess your spiritual growth over the previous weeks. Write this week's verse from memory.

REFLECT: _____

_____

_____

_____

_____

ENJOY GOD'S REST ON DAY 7

WEEK 7 – DAY 1

Have I not commanded you? Be strong and courageous. Do not be frightened,
and do not be dismayed, for the LORD your God is with you wherever you go.
Joshua 1:9

KEEP: _____

_____

_____

_____

_____

_____

_____

WEEK 7 – DAY 2

Have I not commanded you? Be strong and courageous. Do not be frightened,
and do not be dismayed, for the LORD your God is with you wherever you go.
Joshua 1:9

START:_____

_____

_____

_____

_____

_____

_____

_____

WEEK 7 – DAY 3

Have I not commanded you? Be strong and courageous. Do not be frightened,
and do not be dismayed, for the LORD your God is with you wherever you go.
Joshua 1:9

STOP: _____

_____

_____

_____

_____

_____

_____

_____

WEEK 7 – DAY 4

Have I not commanded you? Be strong and courageous. Do not be frightened,
and do not be dismayed, for the LORD your God is with you wherever you go.
Joshua 1:9

DELIVER: _____

_____

_____

_____

_____

_____

_____

_____

WEEK 7 – DAY 5

Have I not commanded you? Be strong and courageous. Do not be frightened,
and do not be dismayed, for the LORD your God is with you wherever you go.
Joshua 1:9

Put into practice the Keep, Start, Stop, and Deliver action items you developed over the past four days based on Joshua 1:9

PRACTICE SCRIPTURE:

Be strong and courageous
1. Being strong means we can withstand great force or pressure. What pressures are testing your strength, and how can you stand strong against them?
2. If you are courageous, you are not deterred by danger or pain. Where do you find courage in times of suffering?

The LORD your God is with you wherever you go
3. Step outside and write down 3-5 objects you see that showcase God's handiwork.
4. Thank God for being with you whenever you step into a new room or building today.

_____

_____

_____

_____

_____

_____

_____

_____

_____

_____

_____

_____

_____

_____

_____

_____

_____

_____

_____

_____

_____

_____

_____

WEEK 7 – DAY 6

Have I not commanded you? Be strong and courageous. Do not be frightened,
and do not be dismayed, for the LORD your God is with you wherever you go.
Joshua 1:9

Reflect on how you incorporated Joshua 1:9 into your life this week, and assess your spiritual growth over the previous weeks. Write this week's verse from memory.

REFLECT: _____

_____

_____

_____

_____

_____

ENJOY GOD'S REST ON DAY 7

WEEK 8 – DAY 1

I wait for the LORD, my soul waits, and in his word I hope.
Psalm 130:5

KEEP: _____

_____

_____

_____

_____

_____

_____

_____

WEEK 8 – DAY 2

I wait for the LORD, my soul waits, and in his word I hope.
Psalm 130:5

START: _____

_____

_____

_____

_____

_____

_____

_____

_____

WEEK 8 – DAY 3

I wait for the LORD, my soul waits, and in his word I hope.
Psalm 130:5

STOP: _____

_____

_____

_____

_____

_____

_____

_____

WEEK 8 – DAY 4

I wait for the LORD, my soul waits, and in his word I hope.
Psalm 130:5

DELIVER: _____

_____

_____

_____

_____

_____

_____

_____

_____

WEEK 8 – DAY 5

I wait for the LORD, my soul waits, and in his word I hope.
Psalm 130:5

Put into practice the Keep, Start, Stop, and Deliver action items you developed over the past four days based on Psalm 130:5.

PRACTICE SCRIPTURE:

Wait for the LORD

1. Find a place of solitude and repeat "Lord I wait for you" for 2 minutes. Then, simply listen for 2 more minutes.
2. Write down 1-5 areas of your life where you are waiting for God. Be honest, and let him know how you feel while you are waiting (e.g., through praise, angry shouts, silence, etc.).

In his word I hope

3. Find a Bible reading plan and look for hope in God's word.
4. The word "hope" is used in the Bible over 300 times. Find some of these verses and pray them as you feel led.

_____

_____

_____

_____

_____

_____

_____

_____

_____

_____

WEEK 8 – DAY 6

I wait for the LORD, my soul waits, and in his word I hope.
Psalm 130:5

Reflect on how you incorporated Psalm 130:5 into your life this week, and assess your spiritual growth over the previous weeks. Write this week's verse from memory.

REFLECT: _____

_____

_____

_____

_____

_____

ENJOY GOD'S REST ON DAY 7

WEEK 9 – DAY 1

Be alert, stand firm in the faith, be brave, be strong. Do all your work in love.
1 Corinthians 16:13-14 (GNT)

KEEP: _____

_____

_____

_____

_____

_____

_____

_____

WEEK 9 – DAY 2

Be alert, stand firm in the faith, be brave, be strong. Do all your work in love.
1 Corinthians 16:13-14 (GNT)

START: _____

_____

_____

_____

_____

_____

_____

_____

_____

_____

WEEK 9 – DAY 3

Be alert, stand firm in the faith, be brave, be strong. Do all your work in love.
1 Corinthians 16:13-14 (GNT)

STOP: _____

_____

_____

_____

_____

_____

_____

WEEK 9 – DAY 4

Be alert, stand firm in the faith, be brave, be strong. Do all your work in love.
1 Corinthians 16:13-14 (GNT)

DELIVER: _____

_____

_____

_____

_____

_____

_____

_____

WEEK 9 – DAY 5

Be alert, stand firm in the faith, be brave, be strong. Do all your work in love.
1 Corinthians 16:13-14 (GNT)

Put into practice the Keep, Start, Stop, and Deliver action items you developed over the past four days based on 1 Corinthians 16:13-14

PRACTICE SCRIPTURE:

Stand firm in the faith
1. Write out your faith story to renew your confidence in God and to keep your faith from wavering (see 1 Peter 3:15).
2. Ask someone to share their faith story with you.

Be brave, be strong
3. God told Joshua to be strong and courageous (week 7, Joshua 1:9). Paul tells the church in Corinth to be brave and strong. How are these commands the same? How are they different?

Do all your work in love
4. Read 1 Corinthians 13:4-7. Write down 3-5 areas where you are not showing love. Now cross out those items and replace them with steps you can take to be more loving.

_____

_____

_____

_____

_____

_____

_____

_____

_____

_____

_____

_____

_____

_____

_____

_____

_____

_____

_____

_____

_____

_____

WEEK 9 – DAY 6

Be alert, stand firm in the faith, be brave, be strong. Do all your work in love.
1 Corinthians 16:13-14 (GNT)

Reflect on how you incorporated 1 Corinthians 16:13-14 into your life this week, and assess your spiritual growth over the previous weeks. Write this week's verses from memory.

REFLECT: _____

_____

_____

_____

_____

_____

ENJOY GOD'S REST ON DAY 7

WEEK 10 – DAY 1

He has shown you, O mortal, what is good. And what does the LORD require of you?
To act justly and to love mercy and to walk humbly with your God.
Micah 6:8 (NIV)

KEEP: _____

_____

_____

_____

_____

_____

_____

_____

WEEK 10 – DAY 2

He has shown you, O mortal, what is good. And what does the LORD require of you?
To act justly and to love mercy and to walk humbly with your God.
Micah 6:8 (NIV)

START:_____

_____

_____

_____

_____

_____

_____

_____

WEEK 10 – DAY 3

He has shown you, O mortal, what is good. And what does the LORD require of you?
To act justly and to love mercy and to walk humbly with your God.
Micah 6:8 (NIV)

STOP: _____

_____

_____

_____

_____

_____

_____

WEEK 10 – DAY 4

He has shown you, O mortal, what is good. And what does the LORD require of you?
To act justly and to love mercy and to walk humbly with your God.
Micah 6:8 (NIV)

DELIVER: _____

_____

_____

_____

_____

_____

_____

_____

WEEK 10 – DAY 5

He has shown you, O mortal, what is good. And what does the LORD require of you?
To act justly and to love mercy and to walk humbly with your God.
Micah 6:8 (NIV)

Put into practice the Keep, Start, Stop, and Deliver action items you developed over the past four days based on Micah 6:8.

PRACTICE SCRIPTURE:

To act justly
1. Research social justice charities available in your town, and consider donating your time or other resources.

To love mercy
2. Listen to Bleed the Same by Mandisa
3. God has given us all mercy, one of his many attributes. Make a list of ways you can show mercy (loving kindness) to others.

Walk humbly with your God
4. Write down a few accomplishments you are proud of. Ask yourself, "Am I proud because of what I achieved, or am I proud because God gave me these opportunities?" Thank God for these accomplishments because he made them possible.

_____

_____

_____

_____

_____

_____

_____

_____

_____

_____

_____

_____

_____

_____

_____

_____

_____

_____

_____

_____

_____

WEEK 10 – DAY 6

He has shown you, O mortal, what is good. And what does the LORD require of you?
To act justly and to love mercy and to walk humbly with your God.
Micah 6:8 (NIV)

Reflect on how you incorporated Micah 6:8 into your life this week, and assess your spiritual growth over the previous weeks. Write this week's verse from memory.

REFLECT: _____

_____

_____

_____

_____

ENJOY GOD'S REST ON DAY 7

WEEK 11 – DAY 1

I have been crucified with Christ. It is no longer I who live, but Christ who lives in me. And the life I now live in the flesh I live by faith in the Son of God, who loved me and gave himself for me.
Galatians 2:20

KEEP: _____

_____

_____

_____

_____

_____

_____

WEEK 11 – DAY 2

I have been crucified with Christ. It is no longer I who live, but Christ who lives in me. And the life I now live in the flesh I live by faith in the Son of God, who loved me and gave himself for me.
Galatians 2:20

START: _____

_____

_____

_____

_____

_____

_____

WEEK 11 – DAY 3

I have been crucified with Christ. It is no longer I who live, but Christ who lives in me. And the life I now live in the flesh I live by faith in the Son of God, who loved me and gave himself for me.
Galatians 2:20

STOP: _____

_____

_____

_____

_____

_____

_____

WEEK 11 – DAY 4

I have been crucified with Christ. It is no longer I who live, but Christ who lives in me. And the life I now live in the flesh I live by faith in the Son of God, who loved me and gave himself for me.
Galatians 2:20

DELIVER: _____

_____

_____

_____

_____

_____

_____

WEEK 11 – DAY 5

I have been crucified with Christ. It is no longer I who live, but Christ who lives in me. And the life I now live in the flesh I live by faith in the Son of God, who loved me and gave himself for me.
Galatians 2:20

Put into practice the Keep, Start, Stop, and Deliver action items you developed over the past four days based on Galatians 2:20.

PRACTICE SCRIPTURE:

It is no longer I who live
1. What does it mean to "die to one's self"?

But Christ who lives in me
2. When you accept Christ as your Lord and Savior, the Holy Spirit is sent to reside in you. How does his presence change your inward view of yourself?

The life I now live in the flesh I live by faith
3. Write down 3-5 ways your life has changed since you accepted Christ and 3-5 ways it has stayed the same.
4. How can your faith help change the items that remained the same?

_____

_____

_____

_____

_____

_____

_____

_____

_____

_____

_____

_____

_____

_____

_____

_____

_____

_____

_____

_____

_____

WEEK 11 – DAY 6

I have been crucified with Christ. It is no longer I who live, but Christ who lives in me. And the life I now live in the flesh I live by faith in the Son of God, who loved me and gave himself for me.
Galatians 2:20

Reflect on how you incorporated Galatians 2:20 into your life this week, and assess your spiritual growth over the previous weeks. Write this week's verse from memory.

REFLECT: _____

_____

_____

_____

_____

_____

ENJOY GOD'S REST ON DAY 7

WEEK 12 – DAY 1

It will be said on that day, "Behold, this is our God; we have waited for him, that he might save us. This is the LORD; we have waited for him; let us be glad and rejoice in his salvation."
Isaiah 25:9

KEEP: _____

_____

_____

_____

_____

_____

_____

_____

Week 12 – Day 2

It will be said on that day, "Behold, this is our God; we have waited for him, that he might save us. This is the LORD; we have waited for him; let us be glad and rejoice in his salvation."
Isaiah 25:9

START: _____

_____

_____

_____

_____

_____

_____

_____

WEEK 12 – DAY 3

It will be said on that day, "Behold, this is our God; we have waited for him, that he might save us. This is the LORD; we have waited for him; let us be glad and rejoice in his salvation."
Isaiah 25:9

STOP: _____

_____

_____

_____

_____

_____

_____

WEEK 12 – DAY 4

It will be said on that day, "Behold, this is our God; we have waited for him, that he might save us. This is the LORD; we have waited for him; let us be glad and rejoice in his salvation."
Isaiah 25:9

DELIVER: _____

_____

_____

_____

_____

_____

_____

_____

WEEK 12 – DAY 5

It will be said on that day, "Behold, this is our God; we have waited for him, that he might save us. This is the LORD; we have waited for him; let us be glad and rejoice in his salvation."
Isaiah 25:9

Put into practice the Keep, Start, Stop, and Deliver action items you developed over the past four days based on Isaiah 25:9.

PRACTICE SCRIPTURE:

We have waited for him
1. Wait: "Stay where one is or delay action until a particular time or until something else happens" (Oxford Languages 2024).
a. Are you waiting for something else to happen before you invite Christ into your life? If so, what are some of the things you are waiting for?
b. Are you waiting for something else to happen before you tell others about God's salvation? If so, what are some of those things?
2. Wait: "Used to indicate that one is eagerly impatient to do something or for something to happen" (Oxford Languages 2024).
a. What are you eagerly impatient to do in your spiritual life?
b. Write down one thing you identified and lift it up to God daily. Revisit the issue at the end of this devotional to assess your progress.

Let us be glad and rejoice in his salvation
3. List the reasons you are glad you have salvation in Christ.
4. Listen to praise music or read hymns of praise for 10 minutes.

_____

_____

_____

_____

_____

_____

_____

_____

_____

_____

_____

_____

_____

_____

_____

_____

_____

_____

_____

WEEK 12 – DAY 6

It will be said on that day, "Behold, this is our God; we have waited for him, that he might save us. This is the LORD; we have waited for him; let us be glad and rejoice in his salvation."
Isaiah 25:9

Reflect on how you incorporated Isaiah 25:9 into your life this week, and assess your spiritual growth over the previous weeks. Write this week's verse from memory.

REFLECT: _____

_____

_____

_____

_____

_____

ENJOY GOD'S REST ON DAY 7

WEEK 13 – DAY 1

And the peace of God, which surpasses all understanding, will guard your hearts and your minds in Christ Jesus.
Philippians 4:7

KEEP: _____

_____

_____

_____

_____

_____

_____

_____

WEEK 13 – DAY 2

And the peace of God, which surpasses all understanding, will guard your hearts and your minds in Christ Jesus.
Philippians 4:7

START: _____

_____

_____

_____

_____

_____

_____

_____

_____

WEEK 13 – DAY 3

And the peace of God, which surpasses all understanding, will guard your hearts and your minds in Christ Jesus.
Philippians 4:7

STOP: _____

_____

_____

_____

_____

_____

_____

_____

WEEK 13 – DAY 4

And the peace of God, which surpasses all understanding, will guard your hearts and your minds in Christ Jesus.
Philippians 4:7

DELIVER: _____

_____

_____

_____

_____

_____

_____

_____

_____

WEEK 13 – DAY 5

And the peace of God, which surpasses all understanding, will guard your hearts
and your minds in Christ Jesus.
Philippians 4:7

Put into practice the Keep, Start, Stop, and Deliver action items you developed over the past four days based on Philippians 4:7.

PRACTICE SCRIPTURE:

And the peace of God, which surpasses all understanding

1. In Alexander MacLaren's Expositions of Holy Scripture, he states, "The peace of God transcends the understanding, as well as belongs to another order of things than that about which the understanding is concerned. You must experience it to know it; you must have it in order that you may feel its sweetness. It eludes the grasp of the wisest, though it yields itself to the patient and loving heart." (MacLaren 1900, Bible Hub)
2. How have you experienced the peace of God?

Will guard your hearts and your minds in Christ Jesus

3. Does this verse refer to our physical hearts and minds, or do you think there is another meaning?
4. How does God's peace guard your heart and mind?
5. If your heart and mind were fully at peace for even a minute, let alone a lifetime, how would you tell someone else to obtain this peace?

_____

_____

_____

_____

_____

_____

_____

_____

_____

_____

_____

_____

_____

_____

_____

_____

_____

WEEK 13 – DAY 6

And the peace of God, which surpasses all understanding, will guard your hearts
and your minds in Christ Jesus.
Philippians 4:7

Reflect on how you incorporated Philippians 4:7 into your life this week, and assess your spiritual growth over the previous weeks. Write this week's verse from memory.

REFLECT: _____

_____

_____

_____

_____

ENJOY GOD'S REST ON DAY 7

WEEK 14 – DAY 1

But I have prayed for you that your faith may not fail. And when you have turned again, strengthen your brothers.
Luke 22:32

KEEP: _____

_____

_____

_____

_____

_____

_____

_____

WEEK 14 – DAY 2

But I have prayed for you that your faith may not fail. And when you have turned again, strengthen your brothers.
Luke 22:32

START: _____

_____

_____

_____

_____

_____

_____

_____

WEEK 14 – DAY 3

But I have prayed for you that your faith may not fail. And when you have turned again, strengthen your brothers.
Luke 22:32

STOP: _____

_____

_____

_____

_____

_____

_____

_____

WEEK 14 – DAY 4

But I have prayed for you that your faith may not fail. And when you have turned again, strengthen your brothers.
Luke 22:32

DELIVER: _____

_____

_____

_____

_____

_____

_____

_____

WEEK 14 – DAY 5

But I have prayed for you that your faith may not fail. And when you have turned again, strengthen your brothers.
Luke 22:32

Put into practice the Keep, Start, Stop, and Deliver action items you developed over the past four days based on Luke 22:32.

PRACTICE SCRIPTURE:

I have prayed for you that your faith may not fail
1. Jesus is talking to Simon Peter in this verse and then informs Peter that he will deny Jesus three times.
   a. If Christ told you that he prayed for your faith, how would that make you feel? How do you think you would respond to Jesus?
2. Write out a prayer for someone's faith to grow and become strong.

When you have turned again
3. Jesus had prayed for Peter's faith, but in this verse, he hints that Peter will fail. He promised, though, that Peter's faith would return.
   a. Write down times you have doubted your faith or doubted God.
   b. Review your list. Were you able to overcome the doubts? If so, how? If not, what will it take for you to turn again?

Strengthen your brothers
4. What are 2-3 ways you can strengthen the faith of your family, friends, or community of believers even when your own faith wavers?

_____

_____

_____

_____

_____

_____

_____

_____

_____

_____

_____

_____

_____

_____

_____

_____

_____

_____

WEEK 14 – DAY 6

But I have prayed for you that your faith may not fail. And when you have turned again, strengthen your brothers.
Luke 22:32

Reflect on how you incorporated Luke 22:32 into your life this week, and assess your spiritual growth over the previous weeks. Write this week's verse from memory.

REFLECT: _____

_____

_____

_____

_____

_____

ENJOY GOD'S REST ON DAY 7

WEEK 15 – DAY 1

"For I know the plans and thoughts that I have for you," says the LORD, "plans for peace and well-being and not for disaster, to give you a future and a hope."
Jeremiah 29:11 (AMP)

KEEP: _____

_____

_____

_____

_____

_____

_____

_____

WEEK 15 – DAY 2

"For I know the plans and thoughts that I have for you," says the LORD, "plans for peace and well-being and not for disaster, to give you a future and a hope."
Jeremiah 29:11 (AMP)

START: _____

_____

_____

_____

_____

_____

_____

_____

WEEK 15 – DAY 3

"For I know the plans and thoughts that I have for you," says the LORD, "plans for peace and well-being and not for disaster, to give you a future and a hope."
Jeremiah 29:11 (AMP)

STOP: _____

_____

_____

_____

_____

_____

_____

WEEK 15 – DAY 4

"For I know the plans and thoughts that I have for you," says the LORD, "plans for peace and well-being and not for disaster, to give you a future and a hope."
Jeremiah 29:11 (AMP)

DELIVER: _____

_____

_____

_____

_____

_____

_____

_____

WEEK 15 – DAY 5

"For I know the plans and thoughts that I have for you," says the LORD, "plans for peace and well-being and not for disaster, to give you a future and a hope."
Jeremiah 29:11 (AMP)

Put into practice the Keep, Start, Stop, and Deliver action items you developed over the past four days based on Jeremiah 29:11.

PRACTICE SCRIPTURE:

"I know the plans and thoughts that I have for you," says the LORD
1. In this passage, God spoke to the Israelite exiles in Babylon through Jeremiah. However, these words can also apply to us individually.
   a. How does this statement from God make you feel and why?
   b. Identify one thing you can do the next time you feel like some part of your life's plan is unclear.

Plans for peace and well-being
2. List 3-5 ways you see God's plans for peace and well-being in your life.
3. Write down an area of your life that lacks God's peace and well-being. Pray about this area every day until you reach the end of this devotional.

Give you a future and a hope
4. Say or write down a prayer request to align your future expectations and hopes with God's will.

_____

_____

_____

_____

_____

_____

_____

_____

_____

_____

_____

_____

_____

_____

_____

_____

_____

_____

_____

_____

WEEK 15 – DAY 6

"For I know the plans and thoughts that I have for you," says the LORD, "plans for peace and well-being and not for disaster, to give you a future and a hope."
Jeremiah 29:11 (AMP)

Reflect on how you incorporated Jeremiah 29:11 into your life this week, and assess your spiritual growth over the previous weeks. Write this week's verse from memory.

REFLECT: _____

_____

_____

_____

_____

ENJOY GOD'S REST ON DAY 7

WEEK 16 – DAY 1

Therefore, as you received Christ Jesus the Lord, so walk in him, rooted and built up in him and established in the faith, just as you were taught, abounding in thanksgiving.
Colossians 2:6-7

KEEP: _____

_____

_____

_____

_____

_____

_____

_____

WEEK 16 – DAY 2

Therefore, as you received Christ Jesus the Lord, so walk in him, rooted and built up in him and established in the faith, just as you were taught, abounding in thanksgiving.
Colossians 2:6-7

START:_____

_____

_____

_____

_____

_____

_____

_____

WEEK 16 – DAY 3

Therefore, as you received Christ Jesus the Lord, so walk in him, rooted and built up in him and established in the faith, just as you were taught, abounding in thanksgiving.
Colossians 2:6-7

STOP: _____

_____

_____

_____

_____

_____

_____

WEEK 16 – DAY 4

Therefore, as you received Christ Jesus the Lord, so walk in him, rooted and built up in him and established in the faith, just as you were taught, abounding in thanksgiving.
Colossians 2:6-7

DELIVER: _____

_____

_____

_____

_____

_____

_____

_____

WEEK 16 – DAY 5

Therefore, as you received Christ Jesus the Lord, so walk in him, rooted and built up in him and established in the faith, just as you were taught, abounding in thanksgiving.
Colossians 2:6-7

Put into practice the Keep, Start, Stop, and Deliver action items you developed over the past four days based on Colossians 2:6-7.

PRACTICE SCRIPTURE:

So walk in him
1. Do "walk in him" and "walk with him" have the same meaning?
a. List a few reasons why you think these phrases may or may not have the same meaning.
2. How does being rooted, built-up, and established in the faith impact your walk in or with Christ Jesus?

Just as you were taught
3. Paul taught Epaphras the good news. Epaphras, in turn, took the gospel to Colossae to teach the people there.
a. Write 3-4 ways that you teach Christ's salvation to others in your life.

Abounding in thanksgiving
4. Write a note or send an email to thank the people who introduced you to Jesus and helped you become rooted in him.
5. Pray a prayer of thanksgiving for the people in your life who shared the gospel with you and lived it out for you to experience.

_____

_____

_____

_____

_____

_____

_____

_____

_____

_____

_____

_____

_____

_____

_____

_____

_____

_____

WEEK 16 – DAY 6

Therefore, as you received Christ Jesus the Lord, so walk in him, rooted and built up in him and established in the faith, just as you were taught, abounding in thanksgiving.
Colossians 2:6-7

Reflect on how you incorporated Colossians 2:6-7 into your life this week, and assess your spiritual growth over the previous weeks. Write this week's verses from memory.

REFLECT: _____

_____

_____

_____

_____

ENJOY GOD'S REST ON DAY 7

WEEK 17 – DAY 1

I will remember the deeds of the LORD; yes, I will remember your wonders of old.
I will ponder all your work, and meditate on your mighty deeds.
Psalm 77:11-12

KEEP: _____

_____

_____

_____

_____

_____

_____

_____

WEEK 17 – DAY 2

I will remember the deeds of the LORD; yes, I will remember your wonders of old.
I will ponder all your work, and meditate on your mighty deeds.
Psalm 77:11-12

START:_____

_____

_____

_____

_____

_____

_____

_____

WEEK 17 – DAY 3

I will remember the deeds of the LORD; yes, I will remember your wonders of old.
I will ponder all your work, and meditate on your mighty deeds.
Psalm 77:11-12

STOP: _____

_____

_____

_____

_____

_____

_____

_____

WEEK 17 – DAY 4

I will remember the deeds of the LORD; yes, I will remember your wonders of old.
I will ponder all your work, and meditate on your mighty deeds.
Psalm 77:11-12

DELIVER: _____

_____

_____

_____

_____

_____

_____

_____

WEEK 17 – DAY 5

I will remember the deeds of the LORD; yes, I will remember your wonders of old.
I will ponder all your work, and meditate on your mighty deeds.
Psalm 77:11-12

Put into practice the Keep, Start, Stop, and Deliver action items you developed over the past four days based on Psalm 77:11-12.

PRACTICE SCRIPTURE:

I will remember the deeds of the LORD
1. Make a list of your favorite Bible stories.
2. Make a list of the circumstances you have seen God work out in your life.
3. God's deeds do not end. His wonders continue throughout eternity, and impact our lives and the lives of each person who was, is, or will be until he comes again.

I will ponder all your work and meditate on your mighty deeds
4. Take one item from each of your lists above and reflect on how God was involved.
5. Were you surprised that God was involved in your personal circumstances? Why or why not?

_____

_____

_____

_____

_____

_____

_____

_____

_____

_____

_____

_____

_____

_____

_____

_____

_____

_____

_____

_____

_____

WEEK 17 – DAY 6

I will remember the deeds of the LORD; yes, I will remember your wonders of old.
I will ponder all your work, and meditate on your mighty deeds.
Psalm 77:11-12

Reflect on how you incorporated Psalm 77:11-12 into your life this week, and assess your spiritual growth over the previous weeks. Write this week's verses from memory.

REFLECT: _____

_____

_____

_____

_____

ENJOY GOD'S REST ON DAY 7

WEEK 18 – DAY 1

Do not use harmful words, but only helpful words, the kind that build up and provide what is needed, so that what you say will do good to those who hear you.
Ephesians 4:29 (GNT)

KEEP: _____

_____

_____

_____

_____

_____

_____

WEEK 18 – DAY 2

Do not use harmful words, but only helpful words, the kind that build up and provide what is needed, so that what you say will do good to those who hear you.
Ephesians 4:29 (GNT)

START: _____

_____

_____

_____

_____

_____

_____

_____

WEEK 18 – DAY 3

Do not use harmful words, but only helpful words, the kind that build up and provide what is needed, so that what you say will do good to those who hear you.
Ephesians 4:29 (GNT)

STOP: _____

_____

_____

_____

_____

_____

_____

_____

WEEK 18 – DAY 4

Do not use harmful words, but only helpful words, the kind that build up and provide what is needed, so that what you say will do good to those who hear you.
Ephesians 4:29 (GNT)

DELIVER: _____

_____

_____

_____

_____

_____

_____

_____

WEEK 18 – DAY 5

Do not use harmful words, but only helpful words, the kind that build up and provide what is needed, so that what you say will do good to those who hear you.
Ephesians 4:29 (GNT)

Put into practice the Keep, Start, Stop, and Deliver action items you developed over the past four days based on Ephesians 4:29.

PRACTICE SCRIPTURE:

Do not use harmful words, but only helpful words
1. Reflect on conversations you have had over the past 48 hours.
    a. Do you recall saying any harmful words, even if they were unintentional?
    b. List those detrimental words, and replace them with helpful words.
    c. Remember to listen first, and then respond with helpful words.

The kind that build up and provide what is needed
2. Write down words that build up others, and work those words into a conversation with 2-3 people today.
3. Consider how you can provide someone with what is needed without using words. Practice this approach over the coming week.

To those who hear you
4. List 3-5 people you haven't spoken to for a while, and call them or meet up with them.
    a. Before talking with them, ask God to fill your mouth with words that will do good in their lives.

_____

_____

_____

_____

_____

_____

_____

_____

_____

_____

_____

_____

_____

_____

_____

_____

_____

_____

WEEK 18 – DAY 6

Do not use harmful words, but only helpful words, the kind that build up and provide what is needed, so that what you say will do good to those who hear you.
Ephesians 4:29 (GNT)

Reflect on how you incorporated Ephesians 4:29 into your life this week, and assess your spiritual growth over the previous weeks. Write this week's verse from memory.

REFLECT: _____

_____

_____

_____

_____

_____

ENJOY GOD'S REST ON DAY 7

WEEK 19 – DAY 1

He must increase, but I must decrease.
John 3:30

KEEP: _____

_____

_____

_____

_____

_____

_____

_____

WEEK 19 – DAY 2

He must increase, but I must decrease.
John 3:30

START:_____

_____

_____

_____

_____

_____

_____

_____

_____

WEEK 19 – DAY 3

He must increase, but I must decrease.
John 3:30

STOP: _____

_____

_____

_____

_____

_____

_____

_____

WEEK 19 – DAY 4

He must increase, but I must decrease.
John 3:30

DELIVER: _____

_____

_____

_____

_____

_____

_____

_____

WEEK 19 – DAY 5

He must increase, but I must decrease.
John 3:30

Put into practice the Keep, Start, Stop, and Deliver action items you developed over the past four days based on John 3:30.

PRACTICE SCRIPTURE:

He must increase
1. Write down 5 ways to strengthen God's presence in your life. How can you put your list into action?

I must decrease
2. Listen to Less Like Me by Zach Williams.
3. Write down 5 ways you can draw closer to God and have others see you as a light in their lives. How can you put your list into action?

_____

_____

_____

_____

_____

_____

_____

_____

_____

_____

_____

_____

_____

_____

_____

_____

_____

_____

_____

_____

_____

_____

WEEK 19 – DAY 6

He must increase, but I must decrease.
John 3:30

Reflect on how you incorporated John 3:30 into your life this week, and assess your spiritual growth over the previous weeks. Write this week's verse from memory.

REFLECT: _____

_____

_____

_____

_____

ENJOY GOD'S REST ON DAY 7

WEEK 20 – DAY 1

Yet this I call to mind and therefore I have hope: Because of the LORD's great love we are not consumed, for his compassions never fail.
They are new every morning; great is your faithfulness.
Lamentations 3:21-23 (NIV)

KEEP: _____

_____

_____

_____

_____

_____

_____

_____

WEEK 20 – DAY 2

Yet this I call to mind and therefore I have hope: Because of the LORD's great love we are not consumed, for his compassions never fail.
They are new every morning; great is your faithfulness.
Lamentations 3:21-23 (NIV)

START: _____

_____

_____

_____

_____

_____

_____

WEEK 20 – DAY 3

*Yet this I call to mind and therefore I have hope: Because of the LORD's great love we
are not consumed, for his compassions never fail.
They are new every morning; great is your faithfulness.*
Lamentations 3:21-23 (NIV)

STOP: _____

_____

_____

_____

_____

_____

_____

_____

WEEK 20 – DAY 4

*Yet this I call to mind and therefore I have hope: Because of the LORD's great love we
are not consumed, for his compassions never fail.
They are new every morning; great is your faithfulness.*
Lamentations 3:21-23 (NIV)

DELIVER: _____

_____

_____

_____

_____

_____

_____

_____

WEEK 20 – DAY 5

Yet this I call to mind and therefore I have hope: Because of the LORD's great love we are not consumed, for his compassions never fail. They are new every morning; great is your faithfulness.
Lamentations 3:21-23 (NIV)

Put into practice the Keep, Start, Stop, and Deliver action items you developed over the past four days based on Lamentations 3:21-23.

PRACTICE SCRIPTURE:

Yet this I call to mind and therefore I have hope
1. List 3-5 people or things that give you hope.
a. Why do you find hope in them?

We are not consumed, for his compassions never fail
2. Write 3-5 things that consume your thoughts, your time, and your resources.
a. God's compassions never fail. What areas of your life do you need to restructure so you are consumed by God's compassions instead of the items on your list?

Great is your faithfulness
3. Meditate on this verse from the hymn, Great is Thy Faithfulness:
"Pardon for sin and a peace that endureth
Thine own dear presence to cheer and to guide
Strength for today and bright hope for tomorrow
Blessings all mine with ten thousand beside."

_____

_____

_____

_____

_____

_____

_____

_____

_____

_____

_____

_____

_____

_____

_____

_____

_____

_____

_____

WEEK 20 – DAY 6

Yet this I call to mind and therefore I have hope: Because of the LORD's great love we are not consumed, for his compassions never fail. They are new every morning; great is your faithfulness.
Lamentations 3:21-23 (NIV)

Reflect on how you incorporated Lamentations 3:21-23 into your life this week, and assess your spiritual growth over the previous weeks. Write this week's verses from memory.

REFLECT: _____

_____

_____

_____

_____

_____

ENJOY GOD'S REST ON DAY 7

WEEK 21 – DAY 1

And I will give you a new heart, and a new spirit I will put within you.
And I will remove the heart of stone from your flesh and give you a heart of flesh.
Ezekiel 36:26

KEEP: _____

_____

_____

_____

_____

_____

_____

_____

WEEK 21 – DAY 2

And I will give you a new heart, and a new spirit I will put within you.
And I will remove the heart of stone from your flesh and give you a heart of flesh.
Ezekiel 36:26

START:_____

_____

_____

_____

_____

_____

_____

_____

WEEK 21 – DAY 3

And I will give you a new heart, and a new spirit I will put within you.
And I will remove the heart of stone from your flesh and give you a heart of flesh.
Ezekiel 36:26

STOP: _____

_____

_____

_____

_____

_____

_____

WEEK 21 – DAY 4

And I will give you a new heart, and a new spirit I will put within you.
And I will remove the heart of stone from your flesh and give you a heart of flesh.
Ezekiel 36:26

DELIVER: _____

_____

_____

_____

_____

_____

_____

_____

WEEK 21 – DAY 5

And I will give you a new heart, and a new spirit I will put within you.
And I will remove the heart of stone from your flesh and give you a heart of flesh.
Ezekiel 36:26

Put into practice the Keep, Start, Stop, and Deliver action items you developed over the past four days based on Ezekiel 36:26.

PRACTICE SCRIPTURE:

A new spirit I will put within you
1. Adding salt to your food or adding honey to your tea enhances the taste.
   a. What is God doing when he adds (puts within) a new spirit in you?
   b. How does this new spirit help you enhance yourself and others?

Remove the heart of stone...and give you a heart of flesh
2. Can a person live with a heart of stone? What causes a heart of stone?
   a. List 1-2 sins that you struggle with the most. In what ways may these sins be turning your heart to stone?
3. A heart of flesh, made and given to us by our glorious God, brings life.
   a. Pray over the sins you listed, and ask God to give you a new heart and a renewed spirit so you may understand the root of these sins.
   b. Live today knowing that God's forgiveness comes with your new heart of flesh. At the same time, you still must constantly battle the sins of this broken world.

_____

_____

_____

_____

_____

_____

_____

_____

_____

WEEK 21 – DAY 6

And I will give you a new heart, and a new spirit I will put within you.
And I will remove the heart of stone from your flesh and give you a heart of flesh.
Ezekiel 36:26

Reflect on how you incorporated Ezekial 36:26 into your life this week, and assess your spiritual growth over the previous weeks. Write this week's verse from memory.

REFLECT: _____

_____

_____

_____

_____

_____

ENJOY GOD'S REST ON DAY 7

WEEK 22 – DAY 1

Likewise the Spirit helps us in our weakness. For we do not know what to pray for as we ought, but the Spirit himself intercedes for us with groanings too deep for words.
Romans 8:26

KEEP: _____

_____

_____

_____

_____

_____

_____

WEEK 22 – DAY 2

Likewise the Spirit helps us in our weakness. For we do not know what to pray for as we ought, but the Spirit himself intercedes for us with groanings too deep for words.
Romans 8:26

START: _____

_____

_____

_____

_____

_____

_____

_____

WEEK 22 – DAY 3

*Likewise the Spirit helps us in our weakness. For we do not know what to pray for as we ought,
but the Spirit himself intercedes for us with groanings too deep for words.*
Romans 8:26

STOP: _____

_____

_____

_____

_____

_____

_____

_____

WEEK 22 – DAY 4

*Likewise the Spirit helps us in our weakness. For we do not know what to pray for as we ought,
but the Spirit himself intercedes for us with groanings too deep for words.*
Romans 8:26

DELIVER: _____

_____

_____

_____

_____

_____

_____

_____

WEEK 22 – DAY 5

Likewise the Spirit helps us in our weakness. For we do not know what to pray for as we ought, but the Spirit himself intercedes for us with groanings too deep for words.

Romans 8:26

Put into practice the Keep, Start, Stop, and Deliver action items you developed over the past four days based on Romans 8:26.

PRACTICE SCRIPTURE:

The Spirit helps us in our weakness
1. You learned last week from Ezekiel that God places a new spirit within you. This same spirit helps you.
   a. Revisit the 1-2 sins you prayed about last week. How do you feel knowing that, as a believer in Christ, God helps you in your weakness?

For we do not know what to pray for as we ought
2. List 3-5 ways in which you can learn to pray. For example, you can study the Lord's Prayer to understand Jesus' direction for your prayers and your life.

But the Spirit himself intercedes for us
3. There may be situations in your life that are so overwhelming you don't know how or what to pray, or may not even pray at all.
   a. Take 5 minutes to meditate on this week's verse, and write down your thoughts about believers receiving help from the Holy Spirit who groans out a prayer too deep for words.

_____

_____

_____

_____

_____

_____

_____

_____

_____

_____

_____

_____

_____

_____

_____

_____

_____

_____

WEEK 22 – DAY 6

Likewise the Spirit helps us in our weakness. For we do not know what to pray for as we ought, but the Spirit himself intercedes for us with groanings too deep for words.
Romans 8:26

Reflect on how you incorporated Romans 8:26 into your life this week, and assess your spiritual growth over the previous weeks. Write this week's verse from memory.

REFLECT: _____

_____

_____

_____

_____

_____

_____

ENJOY GOD'S REST ON DAY 7

WEEK 23 – DAY 1

Restore to me the joy of your salvation and grant me a willing spirit, to sustain me.
Then I will teach transgressors your ways, so that sinners will turn back to you.
Psalm 51:12-13 (NIV)

KEEP: _____

_____

_____

_____

_____

_____

_____

_____

WEEK 23 – DAY 2

Restore to me the joy of your salvation and grant me a willing spirit, to sustain me.
Then I will teach transgressors your ways, so that sinners will turn back to you.
Psalm 51:12-13 (NIV)

START:_____

_____

_____

_____

_____

_____

_____

_____

_____

WEEK 23 – DAY 3

Restore to me the joy of your salvation and grant me a willing spirit, to sustain me.
Then I will teach transgressors your ways, so that sinners will turn back to you.
Psalm 51:12-13 (NIV)

STOP: _____

_____

_____

_____

_____

_____

_____

WEEK 23 – DAY 4

Restore to me the joy of your salvation and grant me a willing spirit, to sustain me.
Then I will teach transgressors your ways, so that sinners will turn back to you.
Psalm 51:12-13 (NIV)

DELIVER: _____

_____

_____

_____

_____

_____

_____

_____

WEEK 23 – DAY 5

Restore to me the joy of your salvation and grant me a willing spirit, to sustain me.
Then I will teach transgressors your ways, so that sinners will turn back to you.
Psalm 51:12-13 (NIV)

Put into practice the Keep, Start, Stop, and Deliver action items you developed over the past four days based on Psalm 51:12-13.

PRACTICE SCRIPTURE:

The joy of your salvation
1. Have you accepted the salvation that comes from the risen Lord? If not, consider accepting Christ by confessing your sins to Him and accepting him as your Savior and Lord of your life.
a. Accepting Christ is not a magic bullet to make your life better. You will still sin, but after accepting Christ, you will also understand what it means to find joy in his salvation.

Grant me a willing spirit, to sustain me
2. List 3-5 reasons why having a willing spirit is important to you and to God.
3. How does a willing spirit sustain you?

I will teach transgressors your ways and sinners will turn back to you
4. When you seek advice, do you turn to someone who has experienced the same or similar situations, or do you talk to someone who hasn't dealt with the same experience? Why?
5. Write down 2-3 ways you can teach others about God's salvation, and how his spirit can restore and sustain. Teach this to someone next week.

_____

_____

_____

_____

_____

_____

_____

_____

_____

_____

_____

_____

_____

_____

_____

_____

_____

_____

WEEK 23 – DAY 6

Restore to me the joy of your salvation and grant me a willing spirit, to sustain me.
Then I will teach transgressors your ways, so that sinners will turn back to you.
Psalm 51:12-13 (NIV)

Reflect on how you incorporated Psalm 51:12-13 into your life this week, and assess your spiritual growth over the previous weeks. Write this week's verses from memory.

REFLECT: _____

_____

_____

_____

_____

_____

ENJOY GOD'S REST ON DAY 7

WEEK 24 – DAY 1

Then you will call upon me and come and pray to me, and I will hear you.
You will seek me and find me, when you seek me with all your heart.
Jeremiah 29:12-13

KEEP: _____

_____

_____

_____

_____

_____

_____

_____

WEEK 24 – DAY 2

Then you will call upon me and come and pray to me, and I will hear you.
You will seek me and find me, when you seek me with all your heart.
Jeremiah 29:12-13

START:_____

_____

_____

_____

_____

_____

_____

_____

WEEK 24 – DAY 3

Then you will call upon me and come and pray to me, and I will hear you.
You will seek me and find me, when you seek me with all your heart.
Jeremiah 29:12-13

STOP: _____

_____

_____

_____

_____

_____

_____

WEEK 24 – DAY 4

Then you will call upon me and come and pray to me, and I will hear you.
You will seek me and find me, when you seek me with all your heart.
Jeremiah 29:12-13

DELIVER: _____

_____

_____

_____

_____

_____

_____

_____

WEEK 24 – DAY 5

Then you will call upon me and come and pray to me, and I will hear you.
You will seek me and find me, when you seek me with all your heart.
Jeremiah 29:12-13

Put into practice the Keep, Start, Stop, and Deliver action items you developed over the past four days based on Jeremiah 29:12-13.

PRACTICE SCRIPTURE:

You will call upon me and come and pray to me
1. Are you as active in your relationship with God as this verse calls you to be?
   a. Call upon me: Take time to cry out to God and ask for his presence.
   b. Come: Be in his presence. From Psalm 46:10, Be still, and know that I am God.
   c. Pray to me: Have a conversation with God about situations and circumstances that weigh on you today. Take joy that he hears you and that you are in his presence.

Seek me with all your heart
2. Describe what it means to seek something with all your heart.
3. Write 3-5 ways you can seek God with all your heart.
4. Take pleasure and rest in knowing that you will find him when you put your whole heart into your search.

_____

_____

_____

_____

_____

_____

_____

_____

_____

_____

_____

_____

_____

_____

_____

_____

_____

_____

_____

_____

WEEK 24 – DAY 6

Then you will call upon me and come and pray to me, and I will hear you.
You will seek me and find me, when you seek me with all your heart.
Jeremiah 29:12-13

Reflect on how you incorporated Jeremiah 29:12-13 into your life this week, and assess your spiritual growth over the previous weeks. Write this week's verses from memory.

REFLECT: _____

_____

_____

_____

_____

_____

ENJOY GOD'S REST ON DAY 7

WEEK 25 – DAY 1

Rejoice in hope, be patient in tribulation, be constant in prayer.
Romans 12:12

KEEP: _____

_____

_____

_____

_____

_____

_____

_____

WEEK 25 – DAY 2

Rejoice in hope, be patient in tribulation, be constant in prayer.
Romans 12:12

START: _____

_____

_____

_____

_____

_____

_____

_____

_____

_____

WEEK 25 – DAY 3

Rejoice in hope, be patient in tribulation, be constant in prayer.
Romans 12:12

STOP: _____

_____

_____

_____

_____

_____

_____

WEEK 25 – DAY 4

Rejoice in hope, be patient in tribulation, be constant in prayer.
Romans 12:12

DELIVER: _____

_____

_____

_____

_____

_____

_____

_____

_____

WEEK 25 – DAY 5

Rejoice in hope, be patient in tribulation, be constant in prayer.
Romans 12:12

Put into practice the Keep, Start, Stop, and Deliver action items you developed over the past four days based on Romans 12:12

PRACTICE SCRIPTURE:

Rejoice in hope
1. How do you define "hope"?
2. The definitions for rejoice all contain the word "joy."
   a. List ways that hope brings you joy.
3. Hebrews 11:1 states, Now faith is being sure of what we hope for and certain of what we do not see (NIV).
   a. Do you believe faith, hope, and joy are connected? Explain why or why not.

Be patient in tribulation
4. On a scale of 1-10, how would you rate your patience when trouble or suffering strikes?
   a. 1 = I scream at God or stay in a fetal position all day; 5 = I can take it, but God, let's not do this again; 10 = Bring it on
5. Use the bookends of this verse—rejoice in hope and be constant in prayer—to help build patience during times of trouble.

Be constant in prayer
6. If you do not have a regular prayer routine, you can start one at any time. Pray at these times.
   a. Before you get out of bed
   b. Before your workday begins
   c. Before every meal
   d. Before every meeting
   e. Before you close your eyes at night

_____

_____

_____

_____

_____

_____

_____

_____

_____

_____

_____

_____

_____

_____

_____

_____

WEEK 25 – DAY 6

Rejoice in hope, be patient in tribulation, be constant in prayer.
Romans 12:1

Reflect on how you incorporated Romans 12:12 into your life this week, and assess your spiritual growth over the previous weeks. Write this week's verse from memory.

REFLECT: _____

_____

_____

_____

_____

_____

ENJOY GOD'S REST ON DAY 7

WEEK 26 – DAY 1

Now, Lord, consider their threats and enable your servants to speak
your word with great boldness.
Acts 4:29 (NIV)

KEEP: _____

_____

_____

_____

_____

_____

_____

WEEK 26 – DAY 2

Now, Lord, consider their threats and enable your servants to speak
your word with great boldness.
Acts 4:29 (NIV)

START:_____

_____

_____

_____

_____

_____

_____

_____

WEEK 26 – DAY 3

*Now, Lord, consider their threats and enable your servants to speak
your word with great boldness.*
Acts 4:29 (NIV)

STOP: _____

_____

_____

_____

_____

_____

_____

WEEK 26 – DAY 4

*Now, Lord, consider their threats and enable your servants to speak
your word with great boldness.*
Acts 4:29 (NIV)

DELIVER: _____

_____

_____

_____

_____

_____

_____

WEEK 26 – DAY 5

Now, Lord, consider their threats and enable your servants to speak
your word with great boldness.
Acts 4:29 (NIV)

Put into practice the Keep, Start, Stop, and Deliver action items you developed over the past four days based on Acts 4:29.

PRACTICE SCRIPTURE:

Consider their threats
1. What threats, real or imagined, keep you from speaking God's word?
   a. How can you overcome these threats?

Speak your word
2. Write a 3-minute testimony that you can use to share God's word, Jesus' sacrifice, and his saving grace with others.

With great boldness
3. List 5 things that will help you give your testimony at home, school, or work more boldly.

_____

_____

_____

_____

_____

_____

_____

_____

_____

_____

_____

_____

_____

_____

_____

_____

_____

_____

_____

_____

_____

_____

_____

WEEK 26 – DAY 6

Now, Lord, consider their threats and enable your servants to speak
your word with great boldness.
Acts 4:29 (NIV)

Reflect on how you incorporated Acts 4:29 into your life this week, and assess your spiritual growth over the previous weeks. Write this week's verse from memory.

REFLECT: _____

_____

_____

_____

_____

ENJOY GOD'S REST ON DAY 7

WEEK 27– DAY 1

Little children, let us not love in word or talk but in deed and in truth.
1 John 3:18

KEEP: _____

_____

_____

_____

_____

_____

_____

_____

WEEK 27 – DAY 2

Little children, let us not love in word or talk but in deed and in truth.
1 John 3:18

START: _____

_____

_____

_____

_____

_____

_____

_____

_____

_____

WEEK 27 – DAY 3

Little children, let us not love in word or talk but in deed and in truth.
1 John 3:18

STOP: _____

_____

_____

_____

_____

_____

_____

_____

WEEK 27 – DAY 4

Little children, let us not love in word or talk but in deed and in truth.
1 John 3:18

DELIVER: _____

_____

_____

_____

_____

_____

_____

_____

WEEK 27 – DAY 5

Little children, let us not love in word or talk but in deed and in truth.
1 John 3:18

Put into practice the Keep, Start, Stop, and Deliver action items you developed over the past four days based on 1 John 3:18.

PRACTICE SCRIPTURE:

Little children
1. Are you insulted or comforted by John using this phrase? Why?
2. Beyond a definition, what does it mean to you to be a child of God?

In word or talk
3. How often do you express your love for another person when speaking with them?
4. The Greek language has seven words for love. Have we, as a society, used the word "love" so casually that it has lost its meaning?

In deed (action) and in truth
5. List 3-5 reasons why acting out love can have more impact than simply saying the word.
6. How can you incorporate acts of love into your life?
7. For love to have its full effect, it must be used in truth. The word "love" should never be used disingenuously. Doing so may hurt another person or may hurt yourself.
8. What does it mean for you to love in truth?

_____

_____

_____

_____

_____

_____

_____

_____

_____

_____

_____

_____

_____

_____

_____

_____

_____

_____

WEEK 27 – DAY 6

Little children, let us not love in word or talk but in deed and in truth.
1 John 3:18

Reflect on how you incorporated 1 John 3:18 into your life this week, and assess your spiritual growth over the previous weeks. Write this week's verse from memory.

REFLECT: _____

_____

_____

_____

_____

_____

ENJOY GOD'S REST ON DAY 7

WEEK 28 – DAY 1

But I have trusted in your steadfast love; my heart shall rejoice in your salvation.
I will sing to the LORD, because he has dealt bountifully with me.
Psalm 13:5-6

KEEP: _____

_____

_____

_____

_____

_____

_____

_____

WEEK 28 – DAY 2

But I have trusted in your steadfast love; my heart shall rejoice in your salvation.
I will sing to the LORD, because he has dealt bountifully with me.
Psalm 13:5-6

START: _____

_____

_____

_____

_____

_____

_____

_____

WEEK 28 – DAY 3

But I have trusted in your steadfast love; my heart shall rejoice in your salvation.
I will sing to the LORD, because he has dealt bountifully with me.
Psalm 13:5-6

STOP: _____

_____

_____

_____

_____

_____

_____

_____

WEEK 28 – DAY 4

But I have trusted in your steadfast love; my heart shall rejoice in your salvation.
I will sing to the LORD, because he has dealt bountifully with me.
Psalm 13:5-6

DELIVER: _____

_____

_____

_____

_____

_____

_____

_____

WEEK 28 – DAY 5

But I have trusted in your steadfast love; my heart shall rejoice in your salvation.
I will sing to the LORD, because he has dealt bountifully with me.
Psalm 13:5-6

Put into practice the Keep, Start, Stop, and Deliver action items you developed over the past four days based on Psalm 13:5-6.

PRACTICE SCRIPTURE:

Trusted in your steadfast love
1. Select verses, people, and stories from the Bible that demonstrate God's steadfast love and your belief in his love.
2. How can you best demonstrate steadfast love?

Rejoice in your salvation
3. In this Psalm, David speaks of salvation from his enemies. Who or what has God saved you from?
4. Rejoice is defined as "to feel or show great joy or delight" (Oxford Languages 2024). Write 3-5 ways you show your delight in God's salvation.

Dealt bountifully with me
5. What does "bountifully" mean to you?
   a. Does God's steadfast love and salvation guarantee us riches, or is there another meaning to this part of the verse?
   b. If you think there is another meaning, please explain.

_____

_____

_____

_____

_____

_____

_____

_____

_____

WEEK 28 – DAY 6

> *But I have trusted in your steadfast love; my heart shall rejoice in your salvation.*
> *I will sing to the LORD, because he has dealt bountifully with me.*
> Psalm 13:5-6

Reflect on how you incorporated Psalm 13:5-6 into your life this week, and assess your spiritual growth over the previous weeks. Write this week's verses from memory.

REFLECT: _____

_____

_____

_____

_____

_____

ENJOY GOD'S REST ON DAY 7

WEEK 29 – DAY 1

But now, this is what the LORD says – he who created you, O Jacob, he who formed you,
O Israel: "Fear not, for I have redeemed you; I have summoned you by name; you are mine."
Isaiah 43:1 (NIV)

KEEP: _____

_____

_____

_____

_____

_____

_____

_____

_____

WEEK 29 – DAY 2

But now, this is what the LORD says – he who created you, O Jacob, he who formed you,
O Israel: "Fear not, for I have redeemed you; I have summoned you by name; you are mine."
Isaiah 43:1 (NIV)

START:_____

_____

_____

_____

_____

_____

_____

_____

WEEK 29 – DAY 3

But now, this is what the LORD says – he who created you, O Jacob, he who formed you,
O Israel: "Fear not, for I have redeemed you; I have summoned you by name; you are mine."
Isaiah 43:1 (NIV)

STOP: _____

_____

_____

_____

_____

_____

_____

_____

WEEK 29 – DAY 4

But now, this is what the LORD says – he who created you, O Jacob, he who formed you,
O Israel: "Fear not, for I have redeemed you; I have summoned you by name; you are mine."
Isaiah 43:1 (NIV)

DELIVER: _____

_____

_____

_____

_____

_____

_____

_____

WEEK 29 – DAY 5

But now, this is what the LORD says – he who created you, O Jacob, he who formed you,
O Israel: "Fear not, for I have redeemed you; I have summoned you by name; you are mine."
Isaiah 43:1 (NIV)

Put into practice the Keep, Start, Stop, and Deliver action items you developed over the past four days based on Isaiah 43:1.

PRACTICE SCRIPTURE:

Fear not, for I have redeemed you
1. Without using a dictionary, write down your definition of redeemed.
2. If God has redeemed you, why should you not fear?
3. List 3-5 ways being redeemed can help you overcome your fears.

I have summoned you by name
4. How well do you remember someone's name after meeting them only once? How do you react when someone calls you by name after meeting you just one time?
5. God not only knows your name, but he calls you by name. How does that make you feel?

You are mine
6. How do you respond when someone you love says, "You are mine"?
   a. Does knowing that God considers you his own bring you peace?
   b. Do you have less to fear when you know that you are his?

_____

_____

_____

_____

_____

_____

_____

_____

_____

_____

WEEK 29 – DAY 6

But now, this is what the LORD says – he who created you, O Jacob, he who formed you,
O Israel: "Fear not, for I have redeemed you; I have summoned you by name; you are mine."
Isaiah 43:1 (NIV)

Reflect on how you incorporated Isaiah 43:1 into your life this week, and assess your spiritual growth over the previous weeks. Write this week's verse from memory.

REFLECT: _____

_____

_____

_____

_____

_____

ENJOY GOD'S REST ON DAY 7

WEEK 30 – DAY 1

Though the fig tree should not blossom, nor fruit be on the vines, the produce of the olive fail, and the fields yield no food, the flock be cut off from the fold and there be no herd in the stalls, yet I will rejoice in the LORD; I will take joy in the God of my salvation.
Habakkuk 3:17-18

KEEP: _____

_____

_____

_____

_____

_____

_____

_____

WEEK 30 – DAY 2

Though the fig tree should not blossom, nor fruit be on the vines, the produce of the olive fail, and the fields yield no food, the flock be cut off from the fold and there be no herd in the stalls, yet I will rejoice in the LORD; I will take joy in the God of my salvation.
Habakkuk 3:17-18

START:_____

_____

_____

_____

_____

_____

_____

_____

WEEK 30 – DAY 3

Though the fig tree should not blossom, nor fruit be on the vines, the produce of the olive fail, and the fields yield no food, the flock be cut off from the fold and there be no herd in the stalls, yet I will rejoice in the LORD; I will take joy in the God of my salvation.
Habakkuk 3:17-18

STOP: _____

_____

_____

_____

_____

_____

_____

_____

WEEK 30 – DAY 4

Though the fig tree should not blossom, nor fruit be on the vines, the produce of the olive fail, and the fields yield no food, the flock be cut off from the fold and there be no herd in the stalls, yet I will rejoice in the LORD; I will take joy in the God of my salvation.
Habakkuk 3:17-18

DELIVER: _____

_____

_____

_____

_____

_____

_____

_____

WEEK 30 – DAY 5

Though the fig tree should not blossom, nor fruit be on the vines, the produce of the olive fail, and the fields yield no food, the flock be cut off from the fold and there be no herd in the stalls, yet I will rejoice in the LORD; I will take joy in the God of my salvation.
Habakkuk 3:17-18

Put into practice the Keep, Start, Stop, and Deliver action items you developed over the past four days based on Habakkuk 3:17-18.

PRACTICE SCRIPTURE:

Yet I will rejoice in the LORD
1. Reflect on the list of failures in these verses. Israel was an agricultural society at this time, so the loss of crops and livestock brought devastation to individuals, families, and communities.
   a. If you lost your job or source of income, would you take time to rejoice in the Lord? Why or why not?
   b. List 3-5 ways you can find the courage and strength to rejoice in the Lord regardless of the hardships in your life.

Take joy in the God of my salvation
2. If God is your salvation, how does this reality help you have joy in good and bad times?
3. Why does salvation make a difference in how you manage difficult or devastating times?

_____

_____

_____

_____

_____

_____

_____

_____

_____

_____

_____
_____
_____
_____
_____
_____
_____
_____
_____
_____

WEEK 30 – DAY 6

Though the fig tree should not blossom, nor fruit be on the vines, the produce of the olive fail, and the fields yield no food, the flock be cut off from the fold and there be no herd in the stalls, yet I will rejoice in the LORD; I will take joy in the God of my salvation.
Habakkuk 3:17-18

Reflect on how you incorporated Habakkuk 3:17-18 into your life this week, and assess your spiritual growth over the previous weeks. Write this week's verses from memory.

REFLECT: _____

_____

_____

_____

_____

ENJOY GOD'S REST ON DAY 7

WEEK 31 – DAY 1

If we confess our sins, he is faithful and just to forgive us our sins and to cleanse us from all unrighteousness.
1 John 1:9

KEEP: _____

_____

_____

_____

_____

_____

_____

WEEK 31 – DAY 2

If we confess our sins, he is faithful and just to forgive us our sins and to cleanse us from all unrighteousness.
1 John 1:9

START: _____

_____

_____

_____

_____

_____

_____

_____

WEEK 31 – DAY 3

*If we confess our sins, he is faithful and just to forgive us our sins and
to cleanse us from all unrighteousness.*
1 John 1:9

STOP: _____

_____

_____

_____

_____

_____

_____

WEEK 31 – DAY 4

*If we confess our sins, he is faithful and just to forgive us our sins and
to cleanse us from all unrighteousness.*
1 John 1:9

DELIVER: _____

_____

_____

_____

_____

_____

_____

_____

WEEK 31 – DAY 5

If we confess our sins, he is faithful and just to forgive us our sins and
to cleanse us from all unrighteousness.
1 John 1:9

Put into practice the Keep, Start, Stop, and Deliver action items you developed over the past four days based on 1 John 1:9.

PRACTICE SCRIPTURE:

If we confess our sins

1. Is confessing your sins optional according to 1 John 1:8-10?
2. How do you confess your sins?

   a. First, you must be saved and accept Christ as your Savior. Once this happens, he gives you the Holy Spirit. John Owen writes in chapter 14 of The Mortification of Sin, "Christ, by his death, destroying the works of the devil, procuring the Spirit for us, hath so killed sin as to its reign in believers, that it shall not obtain its end of dominion." (Owen 2006, 155)

   b. Second, pray that God will make you aware of your sins. Too often, sin is used to justify an end goal.

   c. Third, lay your sins at the cross where Christ died for you (and all mankind) and forgave all your sins.

   d. Lastly, thank Jesus that his sacrifice has made it possible for you to freely confess your sins and receive forgiveness.

To cleanse us from all unrighteousness

3. Reflect on the miracle of this phrase. God loves you so much that the sacrifice of his Son removes all unrighteousness from the Father's sight.
4. As a symbol of your cleansing from all unrighteousness, write down 3 sins that you struggle with. Pray over them and ask God to forgive you. Now, tear the paper into pieces and throw it away. The Holy Spirit has now cleansed you too, but as with any cleaning, things can get dirty again. Repeat this process literally or figuratively every day.

_____

_____

_____

_____

_____

_____

_____

_____

_____

_____

_____

_____

_____

_____

_____

_____

WEEK 31 – DAY 6

If we confess our sins, he is faithful and just to forgive us our sins and
to cleanse us from all unrighteousness.
1 John 1:9

Reflect on how you incorporated 1 John 1:9 into your life this week, and assess your spiritual growth over the previous weeks. Write this week's verse from memory.

REFLECT: _____

_____

_____

_____

_____

_____

_____

ENJOY GOD'S REST ON DAY 7

WEEK 32 – DAY 1

Be wise in the way you act toward outsiders; make the most of every opportunity.
Let your conversation be always full of grace, seasoned with salt,
so that you may know how to answer everyone.
Colossians 4:5-6 (NIV)

KEEP: _____

_____

_____

_____

_____

_____

_____

_____

WEEK 32 – DAY 2

Be wise in the way you act toward outsiders; make the most of every opportunity.
Let your conversation be always full of grace, seasoned with salt,
so that you may know how to answer everyone.
Colossians 4:5-6 (NIV)

START: _____

_____

_____

_____

_____

_____

_____

WEEK 32 – DAY 3

Be wise in the way you act toward outsiders; make the most of every opportunity.
Let your conversation be always full of grace, seasoned with salt,
so that you may know how to answer everyone.
Colossians 4:5-6 (NIV)

STOP: _____

_____

_____

_____

_____

_____

_____

_____

WEEK 32 – DAY 4

Be wise in the way you act toward outsiders; make the most of every opportunity.
Let your conversation be always full of grace, seasoned with salt,
so that you may know how to answer everyone.
Colossians 4:5-6 (NIV)

DELIVER: _____

_____

_____

_____

_____

_____

_____

_____

WEEK 32 – DAY 5

Be wise in the way you act toward outsiders; make the most of every opportunity.
Let your conversation be always full of grace, seasoned with salt,
so that you may know how to answer everyone.
Colossians 4:5-6 (NIV)

Put into practice the Keep, Start, Stop, and Deliver action items you developed over the past four days based on Colossians 4:5-6.

PRACTICE SCRIPTURE:

Be wise in the way you act…Let your conversation be always full of grace
1. Consider your actions when you interact with people outside of the church. Are your actions and words leading people to the gospel?
2. In what ways could someone share the gospel with you that would make you react positively to the message? Write down your answer.
3. In what ways could someone share the gospel with you that would make you react negatively to the message? Write down your answer.

So that you may know how to answer everyone
4. In weeks 9, 16, 17, 23, and 26, you were asked to write your faith story or to discuss salvation with others. Now for the sixth time, write down how you would preach the gospel to someone outside the church.
   a. Compare this to your previous versions. Is it roughly the same or are there significant changes?
   b. How would you tell your salvation story based on your audience (e.g., child, spouse, friend, stranger).

_____

_____

_____

_____

_____

_____

_____

_____

WEEK 32 – DAY 6

Be wise in the way you act toward outsiders; make the most of every opportunity.
Let your conversation be always full of grace, seasoned with salt,
so that you may know how to answer everyone.
Colossians 4:5-6 (NIV)

Reflect on how you incorporated Colossians 4:5-6 into your life this week, and assess your spiritual growth over the previous weeks. Write this week's verses from memory.

REFLECT: _____

_____

_____

_____

_____

_____

ENJOY GOD'S REST ON DAY 7

WEEK 33 – DAY 1

It is the LORD who goes before you. He will be with you;
he will not leave you or forsake you. Do not fear or be dismayed.
Deuteronomy 31:8

KEEP: _____

_____

_____

_____

_____

_____

_____

WEEK 33 – DAY 2

It is the LORD who goes before you. He will be with you;
he will not leave you or forsake you. Do not fear or be dismayed.
Deuteronomy 31:8

START: _____

_____

_____

_____

_____

_____

_____

_____

WEEK 33 – DAY 3

It is the LORD who goes before you. He will be with you;
he will not leave you or forsake you. Do not fear or be dismayed.
Deuteronomy 31:8

STOP: _____

_____

_____

_____

_____

_____

_____

_____

WEEK 33 – DAY 4

It is the LORD who goes before you. He will be with you;
he will not leave you or forsake you. Do not fear or be dismayed.
Deuteronomy 31:8

DELIVER: _____

_____

_____

_____

_____

_____

_____

_____

WEEK 33 – DAY 5

It is the LORD who goes before you. He will be with you; he will not leave you or forsake you.
Do not fear or be dismayed.
Deuteronomy 31:8

Put into practice the Keep, Start, Stop, and Deliver action items you developed over the past four days based on Deuteronomy 31:8.

PRACTICE SCRIPTURE:

The LORD who goes before you

1. Reflect on a time from your childhood when you were in the dark by yourself or got lost.
   a. How did you react?
   b. How do you think you would have felt if you were not alone or if you had someone leading the way in those situations?
2. Moses speaks the words in Deuteronomy 31:8 as part of his announcement to Israel that Joshua would lead them into the promised land.
   a. If you were Joshua—understanding the greatness of Moses, who you now must replace—in what ways would these words bring you comfort?
3. How does this verse comfort you as you take on personal and work tasks today?

Do not fear or be dismayed

4. You may feel fear, anxiety, or distress when you step into a leadership role.
   a. List the reasons why you may have these feelings, and then list ways that God will sustain you.

_____

_____

_____

_____

_____

_____

_____

_____

_____

_____

_____

WEEK 33 – DAY 6

It is the LORD who goes before you. He will be with you; he will not leave you or forsake you.
Do not fear or be dismayed.
Deuteronomy 31:8

Reflect on how you incorporated Deuteronomy 31:8 into your life this week, and assess your spiritual growth over the previous weeks. Write this week's verse from memory.

REFLECT: _____

_____

_____

_____

_____

_____

ENJOY GOD'S REST ON DAY 7

WEEK 34 – DAY 1

But Peter and John answered them, "Whether it is right in the sight of God to listen to you rather than to God, you must judge, for we cannot but speak of what we have seen and heard."
Acts 4:19-20

KEEP: _____

_____

_____

_____

_____

_____

_____

WEEK 34 – DAY 2

But Peter and John answered them, "Whether it is right in the sight of God to listen to you rather than to God, you must judge, for we cannot but speak of what we have seen and heard."
Acts 4:19-20

START: _____

_____

_____

_____

_____

_____

_____

_____

WEEK 34 – DAY 3

But Peter and John answered them, "Whether it is right in the sight of God to listen to you rather than to God, you must judge, for we cannot but speak of what we have seen and heard."
Acts 4:19-20

STOP: _____

_____

_____

_____

_____

_____

_____

WEEK 34 – DAY 4

But Peter and John answered them, "Whether it is right in the sight of God to listen to you rather than to God, you must judge, for we cannot but speak of what we have seen and heard."
Acts 4:19-20

DELIVER: _____

_____

_____

_____

_____

_____

_____

WEEK 34 – DAY 5

But Peter and John answered them, "Whether it is right in the sight of God to listen to you rather than to God, you must judge, for we cannot but speak of what we have seen and heard."
Acts 4:19-20

Put into practice the Keep, Start, Stop, and Deliver action items you developed over the past four days based on Acts 4:19-20.

PRACTICE SCRIPTURE:

Right in the sight of God to listen to you rather than to God
1. Who are you listening to—the lies of this world or the truth of your Lord and Savior?
   a. List 3 ways you can reduce the noise of this world and listen to the gentle whisper of God.
2. Download a Bible app, such as YouVersion, and listen to the Bible for 5 minutes each day.

We cannot but speak of what we have seen or heard
3. When was the last time you told others about God and your faith story, not out of duty, but out of excitement?
   a. What would it take to get you that excited again?
4. Write down the names of 1-3 people you want to talk with about God. Now, do it. Go talk with them.

_____

_____

_____

_____

_____

_____

_____

_____

_____

_____

_____

_____

_____

_____

_____

_____

_____

_____

_____

_____

WEEK 34 – DAY 6

But Peter and John answered them, "Whether it is right in the sight of God to listen to you rather than to God, you must judge, for we cannot but speak of what we have seen and heard."
Acts 4:19-20

Reflect on how you incorporated Acts 4:19-20 into your life this week, and assess your spiritual growth over the previous weeks. Write this week's verses from memory.

REFLECT: _____

_____

_____

_____

_____

_____

ENJOY GOD'S REST ON DAY 7

WEEK 35 – DAY 1

First of all, then, I urge that supplications, prayers, intercessions, and thanksgivings be made for all people, for kings and all who are in high positions, that we may lead a peaceful and quiet life, godly and dignified in every way.
1 Timothy 2:1-2

KEEP: _____

_____

_____

_____

_____

_____

_____

_____

WEEK 35 – DAY 2

First of all, then, I urge that supplications, prayers, intercessions, and thanksgivings be made for all people, for kings and all who are in high positions, that we may lead a peaceful and quiet life, godly and dignified in every way.
1 Timothy 2:1-2

START:_____

_____

_____

_____

_____

_____

_____

_____

WEEK 35 – DAY 3

First of all, then, I urge that supplications, prayers, intercessions, and thanksgivings be made for all people, for kings and all who are in high positions, that we may lead a peaceful and quiet life, godly and dignified in every way.
1 Timothy 2:1-2

STOP: _____

_____

_____

_____

_____

_____

_____

WEEK 35 – DAY 4

First of all, then, I urge that supplications, prayers, intercessions, and thanksgivings be made for all people, for kings and all who are in high positions, that we may lead a peaceful and quiet life, godly and dignified in every way.
1 Timothy 2:1-2

DELIVER: _____

_____

_____

_____

_____

_____

_____

WEEK 35 – DAY 5

First of all, then, I urge that supplications, prayers, intercessions, and thanksgivings be made for all people, for kings and all who are in high positions, that we may lead a peaceful and quiet life, godly and dignified in every way.
1 Timothy 2:1-2

Put into practice the Keep, Start, Stop, and Deliver action items you developed over the past four days based on 1 Timothy 2:1-2.

PRACTICE SCRIPTURE:

Be made for all people, for kings and all who are in high positions

1. Think about your circle of family, friends, and co-workers. Do you have difficulty praying for anyone in your circle?

   a. List 3 of these people and plead humbly (supplication) to God, asking him to intercede in your relationship with them. Also, thank God for each of these people because they are made in his image. Pray for these individuals throughout your completion of this devotional.

2. Below are ways you can pray for local, state, and federal government leaders, and world leaders.

   a. For them to know God and draw closer to him

   b. For them to use godly wisdom when making decisions

   c. For physical, emotional, or spiritual healing

   d. For the peace that surpasses all understanding to abide in them

That we may lead a peaceful and quiet life

3. Joseph Benson writes about 1 Timothy 2:1-2 in his Commentary of the Old and New Testaments. He states, "In the early times the Jews prayed for the heathen princes, who held them in captivity, being directed by God so to do, (Jeremiah 29:7)." And, "The apostle, therefore, agreeably to the true spirit of the gospel, commanded the brethren at Ephesus to pray, both in public and private, for all men, whatever their nation, their religion, or their character might be, and especially for kings. That we may lead a quiet and peaceable life." (Benson 1811, Bible Hub)

4. Pray for peace and wisdom for leaders so that peace can come to your own life.

_____

_____

_____

_____

_____

_____

_____

_____

_____

_____

_____

_____

_____

_____

_____

WEEK 35 – DAY 6

*First of all, then, I urge that supplications, prayers, intercessions, and thanksgivings be
made for all people, for kings and all who are in high positions, that we may lead
a peaceful and quiet life, godly and dignified in every way.*
1 Timothy 2:1-2

Reflect on how you incorporated 1 Timothy 2:1-2 into your life this week, and assess your spiritual growth over the previous weeks. Write this week's verses from memory.

REFLECT: _____

_____

_____

_____

_____

_____

ENJOY GOD'S REST ON DAY 7

WEEK 36 – DAY 1

Let me hear in the morning of your steadfast love, for in you I trust.
Make me know the way I should go, for to you I lift up my soul.
Psalm 143:8

KEEP: _____

_____

_____

_____

_____

_____

_____

_____

WEEK 36 – DAY 2

Let me hear in the morning of your steadfast love, for in you I trust.
Make me know the way I should go, for to you I lift up my soul.
Psalm 143:8

START:_____

_____

_____

_____

_____

_____

_____

_____

WEEK 36 – DAY 3

Let me hear in the morning of your steadfast love, for in you I trust.
Make me know the way I should go, for to you I lift up my soul.
Psalm 143:8

STOP: _____

_____

_____

_____

_____

_____

_____

_____

WEEK 36 – DAY 4

Let me hear in the morning of your steadfast love, for in you I trust.
Make me know the way I should go, for to you I lift up my soul.
Psalm 143:8

DELIVER: _____

_____

_____

_____

_____

_____

_____

_____

WEEK 36 – DAY 5

Let me hear in the morning of your steadfast love, for in you I trust.
Make me know the way I should go, for to you I lift up my soul.
Psalm 143:8

Put into practice the Keep, Start, Stop, and Deliver action items you developed over the past four days based on Psalm 143:8.

PRACTICE SCRIPTURE:

Let me hear in the morning
1. Before you leave your room in the morning to start your day, spend at least 10 minutes:
   a. Kneeling next to your bed and praising God for bringing you into another day.
   b. Reading or listening to Scripture to understand God's steadfast love.

Make me know the way I should go
2. Review your Keep, Start, and Stop entries from this week, and pray over the thoughts you wrote down.
   a. Pray to know God's will, and ask for his guidance and wisdom on how to deliver on those action items.
3. Take 15 minutes to read or listen to the "red letters" in your Bible to understand how Christ calls you to live and how you can answer that call.

_____

_____

_____

_____

_____

_____

_____

_____

_____

_____

_____

_____

_____

_____

_____

_____

_____

_____

_____

_____

WEEK 36 – DAY 6

Let me hear in the morning of your steadfast love, for in you I trust.
Make me know the way I should go, for to you I lift up my soul.
Psalm 143:8

Reflect on how you incorporated Psalm 143:8 into your life this week, and assess your spiritual growth over the previous weeks. Write this week's verse from memory.

REFLECT: _____

_____

_____

_____

_____

_____

ENJOY GOD'S REST ON DAY 7

WEEK 37 – DAY 1

Now faith is confidence in what we hope for and assurance about what we do not see.
Hebrews 11:1 (NIV)

KEEP: _____

_____

_____

_____

_____

_____

_____

_____

WEEK 37 – DAY 2

Now faith is confidence in what we hope for and assurance about what we do not see.
Hebrews 11:1 (NIV)

START: _____

_____

_____

_____

_____

_____

_____

_____

_____

_____

WEEK 37 – DAY 3

Now faith is confidence in what we hope for and assurance about what we do not see.
Hebrews 11:1 (NIV)

STOP: _____

_____

_____

_____

_____

_____

_____

_____

WEEK 37 – DAY 4

Now faith is confidence in what we hope for and assurance about what we do not see.
Hebrews 11:1 (NIV)

DELIVER: _____

_____

_____

_____

_____

_____

_____

_____

WEEK 37 – DAY 5

Now faith is confidence in what we hope for and assurance about what we do not see.
Hebrews 11:1 (NIV)

Put into practice the Keep, Start, Stop, and Deliver action items you developed over the past four days based on Hebrews 11:1.

PRACTICE SCRIPTURE:

Now faith is confidence in what we hope for
1. How does your faith make you certain of what you hope for?
   a. Define what "faith" means to you.
   b. Define "hope in Christ."

Assurance about what we do not see
2. Based on your definition from above, how does faith give you assurance about what you cannot see?
3. List 5 ways you can tell someone how your faith gives you this assurance.

_____

_____

_____

_____

_____

_____

_____

_____

_____

_____

_____

_____

_____

_____

_____

_____

_____

_____

_____

_____

_____

WEEK 37 – DAY 6

Now faith is confidence in what we hope for and assurance about what we do not see.
Hebrews 11:1 (NIV)

Reflect on how you incorporated Hebrews 11:1 into your life this week, and assess your spiritual growth over the previous weeks. Write this week's verse from memory.

REFLECT: _____

_____

_____

_____

_____

_____

_____

_____

_____

ENJOY GOD'S REST ON DAY 7

WEEK 38 – DAY 1

Why are you cast down, O my soul, and why are you in turmoil within me?
Hope in God; for I shall again praise him, my salvation and my God.
Psalm 42:11

KEEP: _____

_____

_____

_____

_____

_____

_____

_____

WEEK 38 – DAY 2

Why are you cast down, O my soul, and why are you in turmoil within me?
Hope in God; for I shall again praise him, my salvation and my God.
Psalm 42:11

START:_____

_____

_____

_____

_____

_____

_____

_____

_____

WEEK 38 – DAY 3

Why are you cast down, O my soul, and why are you in turmoil within me?
Hope in God; for I shall again praise him, my salvation and my God.
Psalm 42:11

STOP: _____

_____

_____

_____

_____

_____

_____

_____

WEEK 38 – DAY 4

Why are you cast down, O my soul, and why are you in turmoil within me?
Hope in God; for I shall again praise him, my salvation and my God.
Psalm 42:11

DELIVER: _____

_____

_____

_____

_____

_____

_____

_____

WEEK 38 – DAY 5

Why are you cast down, O my soul, and why are you in turmoil within me?
Hope in God; for I shall again praise him, my salvation and my God.
Psalm 42:11

Put into practice the Keep, Start, Stop, and Deliver action items you developed over the past four days based on Psalm 42:11.

PRACTICE SCRIPTURE:

Why are you in turmoil within me
1. How often do you reflect on the turmoil (e.g., anger, anxiety, fear, frustration, sin, etc.) that stirs inside you?
2. Every day, or at least once a week, write down any negative feelings you have about specific people or situations.
   a. Review your list and write out why these feelings have taken control.

Hope in God
3. Put your hope in God by praying to him to relieve the troubles you identified in the previous section.

I shall again praise him
4. It can be difficult to praise God when you are suffering through life's difficulties. Yet, the Scriptures provide numerous examples, particularly in the Psalms, of people praising God through their hardships.
   a. Right now, take 3 minutes to praise God for anything good that you can think of. Now take 1 minute to praise him for the turmoil you are in. Doing so may be difficult.
   b. Listen to Praise You in This Storm by Casting Crowns.

_____

_____

_____

_____

_____

_____

_____

_____

_____

_____

_____

_____

_____

_____

_____

WEEK 38 – DAY 6

Why are you cast down, O my soul, and why are you in turmoil within me?
Hope in God; for I shall again praise him, my salvation and my God.
Psalm 42:11

Reflect on how you incorporated Psalm 42:11 into your life this week, and assess your spiritual growth over the previous weeks. Write this week's verse from memory.

REFLECT: _____

_____

_____

_____

_____

_____

_____

ENJOY GOD'S REST ON DAY 7

WEEK 39 – DAY 1

But seek first the kingdom of God and his righteousness, and all these things will be added to you.
Matthew 6:33

KEEP: _____

_____

_____

_____

_____

_____

_____

_____

WEEK 39 – DAY 2

But seek first the kingdom of God and his righteousness, and all these things will be added to you.
Matthew 6:33

START: _____

_____

_____

_____

_____

_____

_____

_____

_____

WEEK 39 – DAY 3

But seek first the kingdom of God and his righteousness, and all these things will be added to you.
Matthew 6:33

STOP: _____

_____

_____

_____

_____

_____

_____

_____

WEEK 39 – DAY 4

But seek first the kingdom of God and his righteousness, and all these things will be added to you.
Matthew 6:33

DELIVER: _____

_____

_____

_____

_____

_____

_____

_____

_____

WEEK 39 – DAY 5

But seek first the kingdom of God and his righteousness, and all these things will be added to you.
Matthew 6:33

Put into practice the Keep, Start, Stop, and Deliver action items you developed over the past four days based on Matthew 6:33.

PRACTICE SCRIPTURE:

Seek first

1. "Seek first" are very difficult words from Jesus. He is asking you (and all of us) to seek first, out of everything else, the kingdom of God and his righteousness. This sounds easy but may be difficult to put into practice.

   a. Do you seek God first when you are in a difficult position or struggle?

   b. To incorporate Jesus' command more fully into your life, seek God first when you rise in the morning and when you lie down to sleep. Also, take time during the day to seek him first by reading or listening to Scripture, and through prayer.

And all these things will be added to you

2. What are these things?

   a. In Matthew 6:25-34, Jesus addressed his disciples' basic needs and reminded them (and you) not to worry. Verse 33 states that the things added to you are food, drink, and clothing.

   b. You may have an abundance of these basic needs, or you may be in a constant state of lack. No matter how your circumstances look, you can thank God for his goodness and faithfulness. He will always make a way for you regardless of your situation.

   c. Write down the things you are thankful for. Then make a point to always seek first the kingdom of God, above everything else.

_____

_____

_____

_____

_____

_____

_____

_____

_____

_____

_____

_____

_____

_____

_____

_____

_____

_____

_____

WEEK 39 – DAY 6

But seek first the kingdom of God and his righteousness, and all these things will be added to you.
Matthew 6:33

Reflect on how you incorporated Matthew 6:33 into your life this week, and assess your spiritual growth over the previous weeks. Write this week's verse from memory.

REFLECT: _____

_____

_____

_____

_____

_____

ENJOY GOD'S REST ON DAY 7

WEEK 40 – DAY 1

Let no one despise you for your youth, but set the believers an example in speech,
in conduct, in love, in faith, in purity.
1 Timothy 4:12

KEEP: _____

_____

_____

_____

_____

_____

_____

_____

WEEK 40 – DAY 2

Let no one despise you for your youth, but set the believers an example in speech,
in conduct, in love, in faith, in purity.
1 Timothy 4:12

START:_____

_____

_____

_____

_____

_____

_____

_____

WEEK 40 – DAY 3

Let no one despise you for your youth, but set the believers an example in speech, in conduct, in love, in faith, in purity.
1 Timothy 4:12

STOP: _____

_____

_____

_____

_____

_____

_____

WEEK 40 – DAY 4

Let no one despise you for your youth, but set the believers an example in speech, in conduct, in love, in faith, in purity.
1 Timothy 4:12

DELIVER: _____

_____

_____

_____

_____

_____

_____

WEEK 40 – DAY 5

Let no one despise you for your youth, but set the believers an example in speech,
in conduct, in love, in faith, in purity.
1 Timothy 4:12

Put into practice the Keep, Start, Stop, and Deliver action items you developed over the past four days based on 1 Timothy 4:12.

PRACTICE SCRIPTURE:

Let no one despise you for your youth

1. Timothy was a very young disciple of Paul. Paul reminded Timothy that age had nothing to do with his ability to minister to others.

   a. Whether you're young or old, you represent Christ to believers and non-believers and can positively impact the lives of others.

   b. List social and cultural factors that may hinder you from proclaiming God's word (e.g., age, personality type, a disability, etc.).

   c. Now consider the people in the Bible, and throughout history, that God has used to proclaim his name. You are not alone.

   d. Review your list of hindrances. Write down ways that God can use these perceived hindrances to reach people with the gospel of Jesus Christ.

In speech, in conduct, in love, in faith, in purity

2. List 1-2 ways you can minister to believers through your speech, conduct, love, faith, and purity.

   a. How will you deliver on your list over the next few weeks?

_____

_____

_____

_____

_____

_____

_____

_____

_____

_____

_____

_____

_____

_____

_____

_____

_____

_____

_____

_____

WEEK 40 – DAY 6

Let no one despise you for your youth, but set the believers an example in speech,
in conduct, in love, in faith, in purity.
1 Timothy 4:12

Reflect on how you incorporated 1 Timothy 4:12 into your life this week, and assess your spiritual growth over the previous weeks. Write this week's verse from memory.

REFLECT: _____

_____

_____

_____

_____

ENJOY GOD'S REST ON DAY 7

WEEK 41 – DAY 1

You are my hiding place and my shield; I hope in your word.
Psalm 119:114

KEEP: _____

_____

_____

_____

_____

_____

_____

_____

WEEK 41 – DAY 2

You are my hiding place and my shield; I hope in your word.
Psalm 119:114

START: _____

_____

_____

_____

_____

_____

_____

_____

_____

_____

WEEK 41 – DAY 3

You are my hiding place and my shield; I hope in your word.
Psalm 119:114

STOP: _____

_____

_____

_____

_____

_____

_____

_____

WEEK 41 – DAY 4

You are my hiding place and my shield; I hope in your word.
Psalm 119:114

DELIVER: _____

_____

_____

_____

_____

_____

_____

_____

_____

WEEK 41 – DAY 5

You are my hiding place and my shield; I hope in your word.
Psalm 119:114

Put into practice the Keep, Start, Stop, and Deliver action items you developed over the past four days based on Psalm 119:114.

PRACTICE SCRIPTURE:

You are my hiding place

1. Life is all-consuming and hard at times, so it's okay if you need to hide and seek solace for a few minutes. The secret is knowing where to hide.

   a. Do not hide and seek solace in worldly spaces, such as in drugs and alcohol, shopping therapy, isolation, or other forms of escapism. Instead, hide in the one and only true Father and his Son, Jesus Christ.

   b. What is your go-to hiding place when life is crashing down around you?

   c. Write down 3-5 ways you can seek the God of hope when you face difficult times. Find your solace in the options you've identified and not in an idol from the world, which often numbs your feelings.

I hope in your word

2. Use a notebook, legal pad, or scraps of paper and write down a Bible verse every day that impacts you.

   a. After a week, review the verses you wrote down and reflect on what they reveal about God's character, yourself, and how you can become more Christlike in your daily activities.

_____

_____

_____

_____

_____

_____

_____

_____

_____
_____
_____
_____
_____
_____
_____
_____
_____
_____

WEEK 41 – DAY 6

You are my hiding place and my shield; I hope in your word.
Psalm 119:114

Reflect on how you incorporated Psalm 119:114 into your life this week, and assess your spiritual growth over the previous weeks. Write this week's verse from memory.

REFLECT: _____

_____
_____
_____
_____
_____

ENJOY GOD'S REST ON DAY 7

WEEK 42– DAY 1

The LORD is my shepherd; I shall not want.
He makes me lie down in green pastures. He leads me beside still waters.
Psalm 23:1-2

KEEP: _____

_____

_____

_____

_____

_____

_____

_____

WEEK 42 – DAY 2

The LORD is my shepherd; I shall not want.
He makes me lie down in green pastures. He leads me beside still waters.
Psalm 23:1-2

START: _____

_____

_____

_____

_____

_____

_____

_____

_____

WEEK 42 – DAY 3

The LORD is my shepherd; I shall not want.
He makes me lie down in green pastures. He leads me beside still waters.
Psalm 23:1-2

STOP: _____

_____

_____

_____

_____

_____

_____

_____

WEEK 42 – DAY 4

The LORD is my shepherd; I shall not want.
He makes me lie down in green pastures. He leads me beside still waters.
Psalm 23:1-2

DELIVER: _____

_____

_____

_____

_____

_____

_____

_____

WEEK 42 – DAY 5

The LORD is my shepherd; I shall not want.
He makes me lie down in green pastures. He leads me beside still waters.
Psalm 23:1-2

Put into practice the Keep, Start, Stop, and Deliver action items you developed over the past four days based on Psalm 23:1-2.

PRACTICE SCRIPTURE:

I shall not want

1. What is David speaking about when he used the word "want?" Does he mean he had an abundance or was he simply content with what he had, big or small?
2. Look back to week 39. Jesus spoke about basic needs that God would provide for his followers. With the Lord as your shepherd, what has he supplied to you so that you do not want?
   a. Is what he has supplied more than the basics? If so, how is it more?

He makes me…He leads me

3. What must we do to allow Christ to be our shepherd and direct our lives?
4. Write down 5 ways you can fully surrender to Jesus.
   a. For each way that you listed, write how these ways may help others put their trust in Christ.

_____

_____

_____

_____

_____

_____

_____

_____

_____

_____

_____

_____

_____

_____

_____

_____

_____

_____

_____

_____

WEEK 42 – DAY 6

The LORD is my shepherd; I shall not want.
He makes me lie down in green pastures. He leads me beside still waters.
Psalm 23:1-2

Reflect on how you incorporated Psalm 23:1-2 into your life this week, and assess your spiritual growth over the previous weeks. Write this week's verses from memory.

REFLECT: _____

_____

_____

_____

_____

ENJOY GOD'S REST ON DAY 7

WEEK 43 – DAY 1

LORD, I have given up my pride and turned away from my arrogance. I am not concerned with great matters or with subjects too difficult for me. Instead, I am content and at peace. As a child lies quietly in its mother's arms, so my heart is quiet within me.
Psalm 131:1-2 (GNT)

KEEP: _____

_____

_____

_____

_____

_____

_____

_____

WEEK 43 – DAY 2

LORD, I have given up my pride and turned away from my arrogance. I am not concerned with great matters or with subjects too difficult for me. Instead, I am content and at peace. As a child lies quietly in its mother's arms, so my heart is quiet within me.
Psalm 131:1-2 (GNT)

START:_____

_____

_____

_____

_____

_____

_____

_____

WEEK 43 – DAY 3

LORD, I have given up my pride and turned away from my arrogance. I am not concerned with great matters or with subjects too difficult for me. Instead, I am content and at peace. As a child lies quietly in its mother's arms, so my heart is quiet within me.
Psalm 131:1-2 (GNT)

STOP: _____

_____

_____

_____

_____

_____

_____

_____

WEEK 43 – DAY 4

LORD, I have given up my pride and turned away from my arrogance. I am not concerned with great matters or with subjects too difficult for me. Instead, I am content and at peace. As a child lies quietly in its mother's arms, so my heart is quiet within me.
Psalm 131:1-2 (GNT)

DELIVER: _____

_____

_____

_____

_____

_____

_____

_____

WEEK 43 – DAY 5

> *LORD, I have given up my pride and turned away from my arrogance. I am not concerned with great matters or with subjects too difficult for me. Instead, I am content and at peace. As a child lies quietly in its mother's arms, so my heart is quiet within me.*
> Psalm 131:1-2 (GNT)

Put into practice the Keep, Start, Stop, and Deliver action items you developed over the past four days based on Psalm 131:1-2.

PRACTICE SCRIPTURE:

Given up my pride and turned away from my arrogance

1. Can pride be healthy? Can it be unhealthy? Why is arrogance always unhealthy?
   a. You can be proud of your accomplishments, your family, even proud of being a Christ follower. However, if pride causes you to put yourself above others, including God, you have entered into arrogance and the sinful position of placing yourself above God.
   b. Recall Micah 6:8 (week 10), which says to walk humbly with your God.

Not concerned with great matters or with subjects too difficult for me

2. This is not a command to shield yourself from intelligent conversations or learning new subjects. However, you must not allow your understanding of these issues to distract you from your relationship with God.

I am content and at peace

3. Are you currently content and at peace? If not, write out the issues that are robbing you of peace.
   a. How can you shift your focus from these issues and set your attention on the peace that comes from God, a peace that surpasses all understanding?
   b. Be content with all that God has blessed you with.

_____

_____

_____

_____

_____

_____

_____

_____

_____

_____

_____

_____

_____

_____

_____

_____

WEEK 43 – DAY 6

LORD, I have given up my pride and turned away from my arrogance. I am not concerned with great matters or with subjects too difficult for me. Instead, I am content and at peace. As a child lies quietly in its mother's arms, so my heart is quiet within me.
Psalm 131:1-2 (GNT)

Reflect on how you incorporated Psalm 131:1-2 into your life this week, and assess your spiritual growth over the previous weeks. Write this week's verses from memory.

REFLECT: _____

_____

_____

_____

_____

ENJOY GOD'S REST ON DAY 7

WEEK 44 – DAY 1

For all that is in the world – the desires of the flesh and the desires of the eyes and pride of life – is not from the Father but is from the world. And the world is passing away along with its desires, but whoever does the will of God abides forever.
1 John 2:16-17

KEEP: _____

_____

_____

_____

_____

_____

_____

_____

WEEK 44 – DAY 2

For all that is in the world – the desires of the flesh and the desires of the eyes and pride of life – is not from the Father but is from the world. And the world is passing away along with its desires, but whoever does the will of God abides forever.
1 John 2:16-17

START: _____

_____

_____

_____

_____

_____

_____

_____

WEEK 44 – DAY 3

For all that is in the world – the desires of the flesh and the desires of the eyes and pride of life – is not from the Father but is from the world. And the world is passing away along with its desires, but whoever does the will of God abides forever.
1 John 2:16-17

STOP: _____

_____

_____

_____

_____

_____

_____

WEEK 44 – DAY 4

For all that is in the world – the desires of the flesh and the desires of the eyes and pride of life – is not from the Father but is from the world. And the world is passing away along with its desires, but whoever does the will of God abides forever.
1 John 2:16-17

DELIVER: _____

_____

_____

_____

_____

_____

_____

WEEK 44 – DAY 5

For all that is in the world – the desires of the flesh and the desires of the eyes
and pride of life – is not from the Father but is from the world. And the world is
passing away along with its desires, but whoever does the will of God abides forever.
1 John 2:16-17

Put into practice the Keep, Start, Stop, and Deliver action items you developed over the past four days based on 1 John 2:16-17.

PRACTICE SCRIPTURE:

The desires of the flesh and the desires of the eyes and pride of life
1. These are desires all people struggle with because they live in a fallen world, one filled with sensual pleasure, covetousness, and vanity.
   a. Choose a desire you struggle with the most, and list 3-5 ways you can guard against it.
2. Read Proverbs 4:23. Consider how your heart controls your life physically, mentally, and spiritually.

Whoever does the will of God abides forever
3. Compare Romans 12:2 to 1 John 2:16-17.
   a. Do you see a connection between these verses even though they were written by two different authors? If so, what connection do you see?
4. Write down 3 ways you can know the will of God.
   a. Do the ways you listed require you to change your daily routine?

_____

_____

_____

_____

_____

_____

_____

_____

_____

_____

_____

_____

_____

_____

_____

_____

_____

_____

WEEK 44 – DAY 6

For all that is in the world – the desires of the flesh and the desires of the eyes
and pride of life – is not from the Father but is from the world. And the world is
passing away along with its desires, but whoever does the will of God abides forever.
1 John 2:16-17

Reflect on how you incorporated 1 John 2:16-17 into your life this week, and assess your spiritual growth over the previous weeks. Write this week's verses from memory.

REFLECT: _____

_____

_____

_____

_____

ENJOY GOD'S REST ON DAY 7

WEEK 45 – DAY 1

You, LORD, give perfect peace to those who keep their purpose firm and put their trust in you.
Isaiah 26:3 (GNT)

KEEP: _____

_____

_____

_____

_____

_____

_____

_____

WEEK 45 – DAY 2

You, LORD, give perfect peace to those who keep their purpose firm and put their trust in you.
Isaiah 26:3 (GNT)

START:_____

_____

_____

_____

_____

_____

_____

_____

_____

_____

WEEK 45 – DAY 3

You, LORD, give perfect peace to those who keep their purpose firm and put their trust in you.
Isaiah 26:3 (GNT)

STOP: _____

_____

_____

_____

_____

_____

_____

_____

_____

WEEK 45 – DAY 4

You, LORD, give perfect peace to those who keep their purpose firm and put their trust in you.
Isaiah 26:3 (GNT)

DELIVER: _____

_____

_____

_____

_____

_____

_____

_____

_____

WEEK 45 – DAY 5

You, LORD, give perfect peace to those who keep their purpose firm and put their trust in you.
Isaiah 26:3 (GNT)

Put into practice the Keep, Start, Stop, and Deliver action items you developed over the past four days based on Isaiah 26:3.

PRACTICE SCRIPTURE:

You, LORD, give perfect peace
1. How do you describe perfect peace?
2. Isaiah 26:1-15 is a song of praise for God's deliverance. Israel had peace from war. Is this an example of perfect peace?
3. Is perfect peace achieved through man or through God? Give a reason for your response.

Who keep their purpose firm
4. In chapter 1 of Rick Warren's book, The Purpose Driven Life, he writes, "You were born by his purpose and for his purpose." (Warren 2002, 17)
5. The NIV and other Bible translations use the phrase "mind is steadfast."
6. Ultimately, you must understand that your purpose is not set by you, but by God.
   a. How does knowing this change your view of your purpose in this world? How does it motivate you to remain steadfast to God's purpose for you?

Put their trust in you
5. List 3-5 ways you have already put your trust in God.
6. List 3-5 ways you can trust God even more.
   a. Is it easier to trust God when you understand his purpose for you? Is it easier to trust him if you know that you can have perfect peace when you do?
7. Pray that the Holy Spirit helps you understand God's purpose for your life and teaches you how to enjoy perfect peace.

_____

_____

_____

_____

_____

_____

_____

_____

_____

_____

_____

_____

_____

_____

_____

_____

_____

WEEK 45 – DAY 6

You, LORD, give perfect peace to those who keep their purpose firm and put their trust in you.
Isaiah 26:3 (GNT)

Reflect on how you incorporated Isaiah 26:3 into your life this week, and assess your spiritual growth over the previous weeks. Write this week's verse from memory.

REFLECT: _____

_____

_____

_____

_____

ENJOY GOD'S REST ON DAY 7

WEEK 46 – DAY 1

And it is my prayer that your love may abound more and more, with knowledge and all discernment, so that you may approve what is excellent, and so be pure and blameless for the day of Christ.
Philippians 1:9-10

KEEP: _____

_____

_____

_____

_____

_____

_____

_____

WEEK 46 – DAY 2

And it is my prayer that your love may abound more and more, with knowledge and all discernment, so that you may approve what is excellent, and so be pure and blameless for the day of Christ.
Philippians 1:9-10

START: _____

_____

_____

_____

_____

_____

_____

_____

_____

WEEK 46 – DAY 3

And it is my prayer that your love may abound more and more, with knowledge and all discernment,
so that you may approve what is excellent, and so be pure and blameless for the day of Christ.
Philippians 1:9-10

STOP: _____

_____

_____

_____

_____

_____

_____

_____

WEEK 46 – DAY 4

And it is my prayer that your love may abound more and more, with knowledge and all discernment,
so that you may approve what is excellent, and so be pure and blameless for the day of Christ.
Philippians 1:9-10

DELIVER: _____

_____

_____

_____

_____

_____

_____

_____

WEEK 46 – DAY 5

And it is my prayer that your love may abound more and more, with knowledge and all discernment, so that you may approve what is excellent, and so be pure and blameless for the day of Christ.
Philippians 1:9-10

Put into practice the Keep, Start, Stop, and Deliver action items you developed over the past four days based on Philippians 1:9-10.

PRACTICE SCRIPTURE:

It is my prayer

1. Describe your prayer life. Are you a prayer warrior? Are you afraid you don't know how to pray? Do you have doubts that prayer even works?
   a. You can always improve your prayer life regardless of how long you've been a Christian.
   b. Jesus says you can ask and it shall be given. Take time to pray for others. Doing so will help you focus on others instead of your own problems and needs, which will keep your troubles in perspective.

Your love may abound more and more, with knowledge and all discernment

2. In chapter 8 of Praying with Paul by D.A. Carson, he writes "the Christian love…is regulated by knowledge of the gospel and comprehensive moral insight…Such love, Paul insists, must abound more and more." (Carson 2014, 106).
   a. List 3 ways that your knowledge of the gospel helps love abound in your life.

You may approve what is excellent

3. Can a sinful person approve of what is excellent or best? If so, how?
4. Focus on the gospel and pray to understand the sufferings Christ endured and his resurrection.
   a. Such focus will help you become more Christlike and compel you to make decisions that are pleasing to God.
5. Pray that your love will abound so that you are pure, blameless, and prepared for Christ's return.

_____

_____

_____

_____

_____

_____

_____

_____

_____

_____

_____

_____

_____

_____

_____

_____

WEEK 46 – DAY 6

And it is my prayer that your love may abound more and more, with knowledge and all discernment, so that you may approve what is excellent, and so be pure and blameless for the day of Christ.
Philippians 1:9-10

Reflect on how you incorporated Philippians 1:9-10 into your life this week, and assess your spiritual growth over the previous weeks. Write this week's verses from memory.

REFLECT: _____

_____

_____

_____

_____

ENJOY GOD'S REST ON DAY 7

WEEK 47 – DAY 1

*Whatever you do, work heartily, as for the Lord and not for men, knowing that from t
he Lord you will receive the inheritance as your reward. You are serving the Lord Christ.*
Colossians 3:23-24

KEEP: _____

_____

_____

_____

_____

_____

_____

WEEK 47 – DAY 2

*Whatever you do, work heartily, as for the Lord and not for men, knowing that from t
he Lord you will receive the inheritance as your reward. You are serving the Lord Christ.*
Colossians 3:23-24

START:_____

_____

_____

_____

_____

_____

_____

_____

WEEK 47 – DAY 3

Whatever you do, work heartily, as for the Lord and not for men, knowing that from t he Lord you will receive the inheritance as your reward. You are serving the Lord Christ.
Colossians 3:23-24

STOP: _____

_____

_____

_____

_____

_____

_____

_____

_____

WEEK 47 – DAY 4

Whatever you do, work heartily, as for the Lord and not for men, knowing that from t he Lord you will receive the inheritance as your reward. You are serving the Lord Christ.
Colossians 3:23-24

DELIVER: _____

_____

_____

_____

_____

_____

_____

_____

_____

WEEK 47 – DAY 5

Whatever you do, work heartily, as for the Lord and not for men, knowing that from t he Lord you will receive the inheritance as your reward. You are serving the Lord Christ.
Colossians 3:23-24

Put into practice the Keep, Start, Stop, and Deliver action items you developed over the past four days based upon Colossians 3:23-24.

PRACTICE SCRIPTURE:

Whatever you do, work heartily, as for the Lord and not for men

1. There is so much packed into this phrase, so let's break it down into 3 areas.
   a. What does "whatever you do" entail? Do you consider God even in the most mundane things you do?
   b. In all you do, do you work enthusiastically, in all sincerity, and in a warm and cordial manner? This is what it means to work heartily. What are a few factors that can motivate you to work heartily?
   c. If you're alive, you work for someone, whether it's a boss, your family, or yourself. However, Paul states we are to work for the Lord and not for others. How does your "performance" for God impact your performance for others?

You will receive the inheritance as your reward

2. What is the inheritance that Paul refers to? How does an eternal perspective change your outlook on all you do?

You are serving the Lord Christ

3. List 3-5 ways that accomplishing your tasks, big or small, to serve and honor Jesus changes your perspective about how you approach everything you do.
4. Take time throughout the day to focus on Christ and the work you are doing. Center yourself in him, and be still and know that he is God. Serve Jesus sincerely and you will naturally serve others.

_____

_____

_____

_____

_____

_____

_____
.
_____

_____

_____

_____

_____

_____

_____

_____

WEEK 47 – DAY 6

Whatever you do, work heartily, as for the Lord and not for men, knowing that from t
he Lord you will receive the inheritance as your reward. You are serving the Lord Christ.
Colossians 3:23-24

Reflect on how you incorporated Colossians 3:23-24 into your life this week, and assess your spiritual growth over the previous weeks. Write this week's verses from memory.

REFLECT: _____

_____

_____

_____

_____

ENJOY GOD'S REST ON DAY 7

WEEK 48 – DAY 1

And let us not grow weary of doing good, for in due season we will reap, if we do not give up.
Galatians 6:9

KEEP: _____

_____

_____

_____

_____

_____

_____

_____

WEEK 48 – DAY 2

And let us not grow weary of doing good, for in due season we will reap, if we do not give up.
Galatians 6:9

START: _____

_____

_____

_____

_____

_____

_____

_____

_____

_____

WEEK 48 – DAY 3

And let us not grow weary of doing good, for in due season we will reap, if we do not give up.
Galatians 6:9

STOP: _____

_____

_____

_____

_____

_____

_____

_____

WEEK 48 – DAY 4

And let us not grow weary of doing good, for in due season we will reap, if we do not give up.
Galatians 6:9

DELIVER: _____

_____

_____

_____

_____

_____

_____

_____

WEEK 48 – DAY 5

And let us not grow weary of doing good, for in due season we will reap, if we do not give up.
Galatians 6:9

Put into practice the Keep, Start, Stop, and Deliver action items you developed over the past four days based on Galatians 6:9.

PRACTICE SCRIPTURE:

Grow weary of doing good
1. List 5 reasons why you might grow weary of doing good.
2. Now, list 8 ways that doing good can revitalize you and others.

In due season we will reap
3. How do you feel when you do not get to see the results of your good works?
4. List 3-5 ways that you know your works are of value even if you do not see the outcome.

If we do not give up
5. Read Psalm 126:5-6. The verses speak of broken and sad people—people who may be weary of doing good—going out to sow seed. Even though they start off sad, each verse ends in songs of joy for the harvest.
   a. Why should you never give up on doing good works? What happens if you do stop sowing (e.g., planting and watering the gospel for others)?
   b. Write down 3 specific actions you can take during the remaining weeks of this devotional to do good works for others. Include actions on your list even if you know you may not see the end result of your deeds.

_____

_____

_____

_____

_____

_____

_____

_____

_____

_____

_____

_____

_____

_____

_____

_____

_____

_____

WEEK 48 – DAY 6

And let us not grow weary of doing good, for in due season we will reap, if we do not give up.
Galatians 6:9

Reflect on how you incorporated Galatians 6:9 into your life this week, and assess your spiritual growth over the previous weeks. Write this week's verse from memory.

REFLECT: _____

_____

_____

_____

_____

ENJOY GOD'S REST ON DAY 7

WEEK 49 – DAY 1

Create in me a pure heart, O God, and renew a steadfast spirit within me.
Psalm 51:10 (NIV)

KEEP: _____

_____

_____

_____

_____

_____

_____

_____

WEEK 49 – DAY 2

Create in me a pure heart, O God, and renew a steadfast spirit within me.
Psalm 51:10 (NIV)

START: _____

_____

_____

_____

_____

_____

_____

_____

_____

_____

WEEK 49 – DAY 3

Create in me a pure heart, O God, and renew a steadfast spirit within me.
Psalm 51:10 (NIV)

STOP: _____

_____

_____

_____

_____

_____

_____

_____

_____

WEEK 49 – DAY 4

Create in me a pure heart, O God, and renew a steadfast spirit within me.
Psalm 51:10 (NIV)

DELIVER: _____

_____

_____

_____

_____

_____

_____

_____

_____

_____

WEEK 49 – DAY 5

Create in me a pure heart, O God, and renew a steadfast spirit within me.
Psalm 51:10 (NIV)

Put into practice the Keep, Start, Stop, and Deliver action items you developed over the past four days based on Psalm 51:10.

PRACTICE SCRIPTURE:

Create in me a pure heart

1. Why does David call on God to create a pure heart in him if he was already a man after God's own heart?
2. Can you have a pure heart on your own (i.e., without God's help)? List at least 3 reasons for your answer.

Renew a steadfast spirit

3. Psalm 51 deals with David's sins against Bathsheba and her husband, Uriah. In this Psalm, David has repented and now calls upon God to renew his spirit.
   a. David raped Bathsheba and then had her husband killed. Is he even worthy to have his spirit renewed?
   b. How would you define "renewal" if you knew someone who had committed such a heinous crime, or if you had done so yourself?
4. Steadfast can be defined as "loyal, firm in belief, and adherence" (Oxford Languages 2024). Based on this definition, what is a steadfast spirit?
5. After you repent from a sin, no matter how big or small it may seem, why is it important to ask God to renew a steadfast (i.e., new and loyal) spirit in you?
   a. How might a steadfast spirit prevent you from sinning in the same area over and over?
   b. Do you pray for this renewal once and then go on about your business, or do you need to revisit this renewal every day?

_____

_____

_____

_____

_____

_____

_____

_____

_____

WEEK 49 – DAY 6

Create in me a pure heart, O God, and renew a steadfast spirit within me.
Psalm 51:10 (NIV)

Reflect on how you incorporated Psalm 51:10 into your life this week, and assess your spiritual growth over the previous weeks. Write this week's verse from memory.

REFLECT: _____

_____

_____

_____

_____

_____

ENJOY GOD'S REST ON DAY 7

WEEK 50 – DAY 1

*Put on then, as God's chosen ones, holy and beloved, compassionate hearts,
kindness, humility, meekness, and patience.*
Colossians 3:12

KEEP: _____

_____

_____

_____

_____

_____

_____

_____

WEEK 50 – DAY 2

*Put on then, as God's chosen ones, holy and beloved, compassionate hearts,
kindness, humility, meekness, and patience.*
Colossians 3:12

START:_____

_____

_____

_____

_____

_____

_____

_____

WEEK 50 – DAY 3

*Put on then, as God's chosen ones, holy and beloved, compassionate hearts,
kindness, humility, meekness, and patience.*
Colossians 3:12

STOP: _____

_____

_____

_____

_____

_____

_____

_____

WEEK 50 – DAY 4

*Put on then, as God's chosen ones, holy and beloved, compassionate hearts,
kindness, humility, meekness, and patience.*
Colossians 3:12

DELIVER: _____

_____

_____

_____

_____

_____

_____

_____

WEEK 50 – DAY 5

Put on then, as God's chosen ones, holy and beloved, compassionate hearts,
kindness, humility, meekness, and patience.
Colossians 3:12

Put into practice the Keep, Start, Stop, and Deliver action items you developed over the past four days based on Colossians 3:12.

PRACTICE SCRIPTURE:

Put on then
1. How can one put on (i.e., wear) the traits outlined in this verse?
2. Paul states in Colossians 3, and in other letters, that upon your acceptance of Christ as your Savior and Lord, you can get rid of your old sinful ways and live according to your new self.
   a. List 3-5 ways people around you know you are living out of your new self.

Holy and beloved
3. Meditate on the reality that as a believer, you are holy and beloved by God.
4. Do you find it easy or difficult to comprehend that the one true and perfect God looks at you as holy and beloved?

Compassionate hearts, kindness, humility, meekness, and patience
5. Write down your definition of each of these characteristics.
6. Choose the one characteristic that is most difficult for you to consistently display to others. Spend the remaining weeks of this devotional praying every day for God to add this characteristic to the patchwork of your new self.

_____

_____

_____

_____

_____

_____

_____

_____

WEEK 50 – DAY 6

Put on then, as God's chosen ones, holy and beloved, compassionate hearts,
kindness, humility, meekness, and patience.
Colossians 3:12

Reflect on how you incorporated Colossians 3:12 into your life this week, and assess your spiritual growth over the previous weeks. Write this week's verse from memory.

REFLECT: _____

_____

_____

_____

_____

_____

ENJOY GOD'S REST ON DAY 7

WEEK 51 – DAY 1

I have stored up you word in my heart, that I might not sin against you.
Psalm 119:11

KEEP: _____

_____

_____

_____

_____

_____

_____

_____

WEEK 51 – DAY 2

I have stored up you word in my heart, that I might not sin against you.
Psalm 119:11

START:_____

_____

_____

_____

_____

_____

_____

_____

_____

WEEK 51 – DAY 3

I have stored up you word in my heart, that I might not sin against you.
Psalm 119:11

STOP: _____

_____

_____

_____

_____

_____

_____

_____

WEEK 51 – DAY 4

I have stored up you word in my heart, that I might not sin against you.
Psalm 119:11

DELIVER: _____

_____

_____

_____

_____

_____

_____

_____

_____

WEEK 51 – DAY 5

I have stored up you word in my heart, that I might not sin against you.
Psalm 119:11

Put into practice the Keep, Start, Stop, and Deliver action items you developed over the past four days based on Psalm 119:11.

PRACTICE SCRIPTURE:

I have stored up your word in my heart
   1. Why is it important to know and understand the words of God the Father and Christ?
   2. Write down ways you can learn Scripture and apply it daily to the circumstances you encounter throughout your life.

That I might not sin against you
   3. How can Scripture help you sin less and increase your desire for a more Christlike life?
   4. Choose 3 verses from this devotional that spoke to you throughout the year and memorize them. If memorization is difficult for you, then write the 3 verses and carry them with you, or put them in a place where you can easily see them.
      a. Memorize, or carry with you, 3 new verses every 3 months.
   5. Let the fire of the Holy Spirit burn bright in you as you get to know the word of God more and more. The common saying is true: it only takes a spark to start a fire.

_____

_____

_____

_____

_____

_____

_____

_____

_____

_____

_____
_____
_____
_____
_____
_____
_____
_____
_____
_____

WEEK 51 – DAY 6

I have stored up you word in my heart, that I might not sin against you.
Psalm 119:11

Reflect on how you incorporated Psalm 119:11 into your life this week, and assess your spiritual growth over the previous weeks. Write this week's verse from memory.

REFLECT: _____

_____
_____
_____
_____
_____

ENJOY GOD'S REST ON DAY 7

WEEK 52 – DAY 1

*In the same way, let your light shine before others, so that they may see
your good works and give glory to your Father who is in heaven.*
Matthew 5:16

KEEP: _____

_____

_____

_____

_____

_____

_____

_____

WEEK 52 – DAY 2

*In the same way, let your light shine before others, so that they may see
your good works and give glory to your Father who is in heaven.*
Matthew 5:16

START: _____

_____

_____

_____

_____

_____

_____

_____

WEEK 52 – DAY 3

*In the same way, let your light shine before others, so that they may see
your good works and give glory to your Father who is in heaven.*
Matthew 5:16

STOP: _____

_____

_____

_____

_____

_____

_____

_____

_____

WEEK 52 – DAY 4

*In the same way, let your light shine before others, so that they may see
your good works and give glory to your Father who is in heaven.*
Matthew 5:16

DELIVER: _____

_____

_____

_____

_____

_____

_____

_____

_____

WEEK 52 – DAY 5

In the same way, let your light shine before others, so that they may see
your good works and give glory to your Father who is in heaven.
Matthew 5:16

Put into practice the Keep, Start, Stop, and Deliver action items you developed over the past four days based on Matthew 5:16.

PRACTICE SCRIPTURE:

Let your light shine before others
1. You are now God's light on this earth. Why is it important to let your light shine and burn?
2. List 3-5 ways you can shine your light to both believers and nonbelievers.
3. Listen to Burn Baby Burn by MercyMe.

They may see your good works
4. Why is it important that others see your good works?
5. Does your light shine due to your good works or because of God's grace?

Give glory to your Father
6. To give glory is to praise. Spend the next 3 minutes praising God for his salvation plan and for all that you have, knowing it is all from him.

_____

_____

_____

_____

_____

_____

_____

_____

_____

_____

_____
_____
_____
_____
_____
_____
_____
_____
_____
_____

WEEK 52 – DAY 6

In the same way, let your light shine before others, so that they may see
your good works and give glory to your Father who is in heaven.
Matthew 5:16

Reflect on how you incorporated Matthew 5:16 into your life this week, and assess your spiritual growth over the previous weeks. Write this week's verse from memory.

REFLECT: _____

_____

_____

_____

_____

ENJOY GOD'S REST ON DAY 7

SOURCES

Bible Hub. "1 Timothy 2." Joseph Benson's Commentary of the Old and New Testaments. Accessed April 12, 2024; "Philippians 4." Alexander MacLaren's Expositions of Holy Scripture. Accessed April 12, 2024.

Carson, D.A. Praying with Paul: A Call to Spiritual Reformation. Grand Rapids, MI: Baker Publishing Group, 2014.

Chisholm, Thomas, William M. Runyan. "Great is Thy Faithfulness." Hope Publishing, 1923.

Oxford Languages, s.v. "rejoice (v.)," "steadfast (adj.)," "wait (v.)," accessed April 11, 2024.

Owen, John. The Mortification of Sin. Geanies House, Fearn, Ross-shire, Scotland, United Kingdom: Christian Focus Publications, 2006.

Warren, Rick. The Purpose Driven Life. Grand Rapids, MI: Zondervan, 2002.

About the Author

Todd Crippin has had an active faith throughout his life even when he felt like a poser within his outward Christian life. Living dual lives at times, he still desired to know God better. Through his wife and children, Todd began to bring his faith into focus again. Fixated on living an active faith, he began involving himself in his church community and searching for God through prayer and scripture. Coupling this with a strong desire to serve as light to his co-workers and others he met, he began to search for ways to incorporate his faith into his professional life. This led to viewing professional and personal lives as one. From this, the idea of taking corporate concepts and practices and incorporating them into studying the Bible. Having always found comfort in Christian devotions, Todd decided to create a devotional that created an active approach in understanding how a verse(s) is applying to him. Please join Todd on his journey at activedevotional.com and @activedevotionals1965 on YouTube.